The Changing Currents of Transpacific Integration

THE CHANGING CURRENTS OF Transpacific Integration

China, the TPP, and Beyond

edited by
Adrian H. Hearn
Margaret Myers

LYNNE RIENNER PUBLISHERS
BOULDER
LONDON

Published in the United States of America in 2017 by
Lynne Rienner Publishers, Inc.
1800 30th Street, Boulder, Colorado 80301
www.rienner.com

and in the United Kingdom by
Lynne Rienner Publishers, Inc.
3 Henrietta Street, Covent Garden, London WC2E 8LU

Library of Congress Cataloging-in-Publication Data
A Cataloging-in-Publication record for this book
is available from the Library of Congress.

ISBN 978-1-62637-564-2

British Cataloguing in Publication Data
A Cataloguing in Publication record for this book
is available from the British Library.

Printed and bound in the United States of America

The paper used in this publication meets the requirements
of the American National Standard for Permanence of
Paper for Printed Library Materials Z39.48-1992.

5 4 3 2 1

Contents

Foreword

Carla A. Hills

TRADE PATTERNS HAVE CHANGED DRAMATICALLY IN THE PAST two decades. The intensity of economic growth has shifted from the West to the East. Increasingly, supply chains encircle the globe, linking developed and developing countries in recognition of the fact that today emerging economies account for a majority of global growth. Regional trade arrangements have proliferated worldwide, but nowhere more so than in Asia. A decade ago there were roughly sixty trade agreements in the region; today there are five times that many. Negotiations involving multiple nations continue.

One of the most significant emerging agreements is the Trans-Pacific Partnership (TPP), which stretches across the Pacific connecting nations in Asia with those in the Western Hemisphere. What began in 2006 as an agreement involving Brunei, Chile, New Zealand, and Singapore has expanded and now includes twelve nations: the original four plus Australia, Canada, Japan, Malaysia, Mexico, Peru, the United States, and Vietnam. These nations account for roughly 40 percent of global gross domestic product and one-third of global trade. Their aim is to achieve a comprehensive and high-level agreement that attains a broader opening of markets than did prior trade agreements and will serve as a template for future trade agreements. Negotiations cover a range of activities including the commercial operations of state-owned enterprises, protection of intellectual property, services, and government procurement.

At the same time, China is negotiating the Regional Comprehensive Economic Partnership (RCEP) with the ten nations that compose the Association of Southeast Asian Nations (ASEAN) (Brunei, Cambodia, Indonesia, Laos, Malaysia, Myanmar, Philippines, Singapore, Thailand, and Vietnam) plus the six nations with which ASEAN has existing trade agreements (Australia, China, India, Japan, South Korea, and New Zealand). The ambition is to promote regional economic integration in East Asia. Six Asian nations are participating in the negotiations of both the TPP and RCEP.

But the world's two largest economies, China and the United States, are proceeding separately: the United States in the TPP and China in RCEP. That raises questions of whether the parallel trade efforts will help bring the parties together or pull them apart. Some Western scholars have suggested that China is promoting RCEP to create a regional economic integration in East Asia that will exclude the United States, whereas some Chinese scholars have suggested that US efforts in negotiating the TPP are motivated by a desire to reduce China's influence in East Asia. While arguments can be made that neither suggestion is well grounded in facts underlying the origins of the respective negotiations, perceptions matter.

In this volume, Adrian H. Hearn and Margaret Myers have assembled a group of authors, whom they join, to present their perceptions of the TPP, RCEP, and US-China relations. They not only describe the differing views that exist regarding the merits of these two trade negotiations, but also share their respective assessments of the likely impact these agreements could have in terms of political and economic integration in Asia and Latin America. The resulting analyses of challenges and opportunities constitute a timely and useful presentation, not least as debates about the TPP, China, and the changing currents of transpacific integration intensify within the United States.

The Changing Currents of Transpacific Integration

1

Regional Integration or Disintegration?

Adrian H. Hearn and Margaret Myers

FEW DEVELOPMENTS IN THE ASIA PACIFIC REGION HAVE SIMULTANEOUSLY harbored such opportunity and such risk as the Trans-Pacific Partnership (TPP). The TPP is the centerpiece of the US "pivot" to Asia, and 35 percent of global trade is represented by its twelve members: Australia, Brunei, Canada, Chile, Japan, Malaysia, Mexico, New Zealand, Peru, Singapore, the United States, and Vietnam. Economic projections of the TPP's impact vary: one widely quoted study by Peter Petri, Michael Plummer, and Fan Zhai (2012) estimates global gains of $295 billion; while the United Nations Global Policy Model, employed by Jeronim Capaldo, Alex Izurieta, and Jomo Kwame Sundaram (2016), finds that after ten years the TPP would produce negligible growth and 771,000 job losses. The agreement's policy implications are no less controversial. No prior multilateral proposal has set its sights so far "behind the borders" of signatories to regulate investment, intellectual property, and state-owned enterprises (SOEs). Its wide-ranging implications for labor standards, social services, and freedom of online data portend a comprehensive blueprint for future agreements. And yet, the TPP's assertive vision of Asia Pacific integration may harbor the seeds of regional disintegration.

The TPP's core goal is also its greatest liability: it seeks to expand the role of markets in the delivery of healthcare, housing, foreign investment, and services in a region where government programs have long underpinned social welfare, national development, and international cooperation. Vietnam stands out among TPP members for its high level of state intervention, but more significant for the region's trajectory is China, where the encompassing role of the state in practically all aspects of national and foreign affairs preempts TPP membership (Lim, Elms, and Low 2012). As Eric Stadius and Elizabeth Briggs write, "Beijing's policy of sustaining state run enterprises, the difficulties surrounding land purchase in China, the Chinese Central Bank's intentional undervaluation of the currency, and various barriers to free trade all violate the principles of the TPP" (2012). Chinese currency manipulation, writes C. Fred Bergsten, has cost the US economy "several hundred billion dollars" and "several million additional jobs" and should therefore be countered through the TPP:

> Currency manipulation is, by far, the world's most protectionist international economic policy in the 21st century, but neither the U.S. government nor the responsible international institutions, the International Monetary Fund and the World Trade Organization, have mounted effective responses. Congress has therefore been expressing great concern over the issue and wants to take the occasion of the forthcoming legislation on new U.S. trade agreements, most notably the Trans-Pacific Partnership (TPP), to promote decisive counteraction. (Bergsten 2015)

To the dismay of many in Congress, the TPP contains no enforceable provisions on currency manipulation. Its guidelines on enhanced transparency and reporting of exchange-rate policies are therefore unlikely to generate a regional environment that would deter China from further devaluing the renminbi, as it did in August 2015.

While the TPP cannot impede currency manipulation in member nations, much less in China, it has provoked criticism from Chinese commentators. Most paint a somber picture of the TPP, noting that trade is already relatively open between its members and that it is therefore likely to harbor ulterior motives. According to Cai Penghong (2011), director of the Asia Pacific Economic Cooperation (APEC) Research Center at the Shanghai Academy of Social Sciences: "It seems that the U.S. is using the TPP as a tool as a part of its Asia Pacific Strategy to contain China." The agreement is also described as a US-led plan to undermine ASEAN+3 (Association of Southeast Asian Nations), an institution that has leveraged China's growth to consolidate East Asian economic integration (Li 2012). A prominent foreign contributor to Chinese official media, John Ross (2011), argues that the TPP aims "to reorient trade discussion in the Pacific away from the most dynamic market, China, to the less dynamic one of the U.S. by setting terms which exclude China." Similarly, according to K. V. Kesavan and Kartikeya Khanna (2012), "the partnership serves to compete with China's economic interests rather than be complementary."

Interviews conducted in Beijing between 2012 and 2015 by this volume's editors confirm that Chinese researchers and policy advisers are uncomfortable with the TPP. For instance, Han Feng, deputy director of the Asia Pacific Institute at the Chinese Academy of Social Sciences, described a concern among Chinese foreign policy advisers that the TPP may seek to eventually incorporate Taiwan and therefore pose a threat to Chinese sovereignty. Wang Honggang, deputy director of US studies at the China Institute of Contemporary International Relations, noted a widely shared suspicion that the US government is using the TPP negotiations to limit China's international expansion. Similarly, Di Dongsheng, deputy director of the Renmin University Center for Chinese Foreign Strategy Studies, suggested that the TPP's high but unrealistic standards are supportive of US economic goals and afford China only a "take it or leave it" option. Pan Wei, director of the Center for Chinese and Global Affairs at Peking University, asserted that influential TPP signatories such as Australia should advocate the redrafting of controversial chapters of the agreement to facilitate China's membership. In general, Chinese officials are worried that the TPP will entrench divisions between Asia Pacific nations favorable to US interests on the one hand, and those sympathetic to China on the other.

The Taiwan question epitomizes the TPP's political nature, because, as Han Feng suggested, it is inextricable from the sensitive diplomacy of the One China Policy. Taiwan's government under Ma Ying-jeou of the Kuomintang (2008–2016), like other Asia Pacific governments, believed that the TPP could create a regional environment that would facilitate its pursuit of domestic economic reforms. But as Shihoko Goto (2015) writes: "Given its experience in joining the World Trade Organization, whereby it had to wait until China was ready for accession in 2001 so that it could join at the same time, there is growing concern that Taipei would have to wait again for Beijing to be ready." To join the TPP without Beijing's consent would constitute an unprecedented assertion of political autonomy; it would also put unwanted pressure on TPP members to articulate a position on Taiwan's sovereign status. These circumstances have become more likely with the January 2016 election of Tsai Ing-wen of the Democratic Progressive Party, which has previously advocated greater independence from mainland China. The TPP provides Taiwan's new government an opportunity to assert its autonomy, binding the dynamics of cross-Strait relations to the broader debate over the agreement's potential to propel the Asia Pacific region toward integration or disintegration.

In the chapters that follow, the authors find no hard evidence that the TPP seeks to contain or curtail Chinese interests, though its unusually broad remit and apparent resonance with US strategic priorities have understandably provoked suspicions in Beijing. This sentiment has been aggravated by US political rhetoric, including President Barack Obama's attempt to build domestic support for the TPP: "95% of the world's potential customers live outside our borders. Many of them live in the Asia Pacific—the world's fastest-growing region. And as we speak, China is trying to write the rules for trade in the 21st century. That would put our workers and our businesses at a massive disadvantage. We can't let that happen. We should write those rules" (White House 2015). This is a subtle remark compared to US secretary of defense Ashton Carter's statement prior to visiting Japan and South

Korea: "Passing TPP is as important to me as another aircraft carrier . . . it would help us promote a global order that reflects both our interests and our values" (Carter 2015). Intentionally or not, the statement implies coercive unilateralism, playing into the hands of TPP critics. As Sam Roggeveen (2015) of the Lowy Institute for International Policy writes: "It's a soundbite tailor made for those Beijing skeptics who see the TPP as a device which deliberately excludes them, and which functions as the economic component of a U.S.-led China containment strategy."

Commitments by senior officials to internationalizing US "interests and values" may galvanize domestic audiences, but listeners around the world find this rhetoric unsophisticated and sometimes overbearing. A more nuanced message would focus on shared interests and values, and how agreements like the TPP can advance them. As several of the volume's chapters point out, senior Chinese politicians are currently promoting market reforms and more liberal foreign investment conditions that resonate with TPP goals. The zero-sum language employed by some US officials generates unnecessary foreign anxiety about irreconcilable differences, forceful unilateralism, and the militarization of relationships that are concerned less with strategic posturing than with economic exchange.

While the friction generated by nationalistic statements can be easily avoided, previous US commercial partnerships have in some cases developed a military dimension. This phenomenon is evident in the post-9/11 Security and Prosperity Partnership negotiated by the countries of the North American Free Trade Agreement (NAFTA), and its subsequent evolution into Plan Mexico (also known as the Merida Initiative). Resulting in augmented US military presence in Mexico, the emerging trade-security nexus was articulated by former US assistant secretary of state for Western Hemisphere affairs Thomas Shannon: "We have worked through the Security and Prosperity Partnership to improve our commercial and trading relationship, we have also worked to improve our security cooperation. To a certain extent, we're armoring NAFTA" (quoted in Fitzpatrick Behrens 2009). Nobody has formally advocated "armoring the TPP," but the prospect is plausible as China stakes increasingly assertive maritime claims and races to install "multi-use" landing strips and port infrastructure in contested territories.

Power and Money in the Asia Pacific

While Chinese strategic capabilities in East Asia do not (yet) rival those of the United States, the financial picture is changing more quickly. The China Development Bank and the Export Import Bank of China now provide more loans to the region than the World Bank and the Asian Development Bank combined. Similarly, research from the Inter-American Dialogue shows that Chinese loans to Latin America have exceeded the combined loans of the World Bank, the Inter-American Development Bank, and the US Export Import Bank to the region since 2010 (Gallagher and Myers 2014).

Kevin Gallagher (2015) compares the significance of China's global distribution of finance to US investment in European reconstruction after World War II: "China-backed finance has the potential to be nothing short of a 21st century Marshall Plan." Supporting this conclusion, the China-led Asian Infrastructure Investment Bank (AIIB)—criticized by the United States for its questionable governance standards but widely embraced in Europe and Asia—has established an initial fund of $50 billion ($100 billion including call-in capital) for regional development.

The AIIB's capacity to advance Chinese policy interests, such as opening export markets, is a key point of contention. As Sun Yun writes, "Promoting exports of Chinese goods to absorb excess capacity runs the risks of encouraging anti-dumping lawsuits, undermining Xi's economic restructuring campaign and, more importantly, undermining the AIIB's legitimacy and credibility" (2015: 1–2). And yet a senior researcher at the National Development and Reform Commission (NDRC) has acknowledged that the AIIB's agenda is something other than commercial: "the operation of the AIIB will not seek high returns but rather to break even or earn minimal profits" (quoted in Yun 2015: 2). The AIIB's instigators thus appear to be less concerned with short-term profitability than with creating a regional environment conducive to Chinese infrastructure investment and diplomatic engagement. These objectives resemble the goals of other recent Chinese initiatives, such as the Silk Road Fund, which has earmarked $46 billion for Central Asian port development, rail and road links, and power generation (coal, wind, solar, and hydro), and the New Development Bank, which the BRICS bloc (Brazil, Russia, India, China, and South Africa), spearheaded by China, launched in 2014 with initial capital of $100 billion.

As they contend with dominant structures of finance and governance, Chinese loans and investments have inevitably generated tensions. Many of these tensions can be traced to a core disagreement over the merits of free market and state-led development. The TPP sits at the epicenter of this debate. Derek Scissors of the Heritage Foundation argues that, at a time when Chinese government enterprises are investing overseas like never before, the TPP can ensure a competitive world market: "The outlook for Chinese investment is positive, but setbacks will continue to occur, due in part to foreign suspicion of state firms. The U.S. should formulate policy to ensure competition, with the Chinese firms that come here, in the Chinese market, and around the world through the Trans-Pacific Partnership and other agreements that liberalize market access" (2013a: 1). The TPP's gravity, as Scissors implies, resides in its aspiration to extend prevailing market economy conditions, and the opportunities they bring for private enterprise, around the world and potentially into China. Since China is not party to the TPP negotiations and is unlikely to meet its conditions in the foreseeable future—much less in light of the Xi Jinping administration's defense of SOEs—the liberalization agenda focuses for the time being on China's neighbors.

As noted earlier, infrastructure, industry, and social services in many Southeast Asian nations depend on direct support from government budgets and increasingly on investment from the Chinese state. This injection of Chinese finance is mutually beneficial: the exports it fuels from recipient countries are increasingly bound for China, filling the lower rungs of Chinese production chains and propelling them into more sophisticated and profitable sectors. This symbiosis emerged in force after the 1997 Asian financial crisis and accelerated a decade later with the global financial crisis. The latest wave of Chinese outbound finance, channeled through the AIIB and Silk Road Fund, aims to inject further capital into regional development while consolidating China's leadership.

Any disruption to the flow of Chinese finance, for instance through a commitment among TPP signatories to favor inbound investment from private rather than public sectors, would alter the trajectory of Asian integration. It stands to reason, then, that China and its neighbors are hedging against the TPP by negotiating parallel free trade agreements (FTAs) with each other. China has already signed bilateral FTAs with TPP members Australia, Chile, New Zealand, Peru, and Singapore; has joined a multilateral FTA (via ASEAN) with TPP members Malaysia, Brunei, and Vietnam; and is seeking further Asia Pacific FTAs. As Chapters 5 and 6 explain, China has worked hard to consolidate these networks by advocating the conclusion of two multilateral initiatives: the Comprehensive Economic Partnership for East Asia (CEPEA, originally proposed by Japan) and the East Asia Free Trade Area (EAFTA, based on ASEAN+3). Largely through China's efforts, in 2012 the negotiations for these two frameworks were combined under the Regional Comprehensive Economic Partnership (RCEP), whose members include Australia, Brunei, Cambodia, China, Indonesia, Japan, Laos, Malaysia, Myanmar, New Zealand, the Philippines, Singapore, South Korea, Thailand, and Vietnam.

For economist Jianmin Jin (2013), "the sudden rise of the RCEP is in fact due to the many concerns Asia has about the TPP"; and as Han Feng stated in an interview (24 September 2012), "the RCEP agreement is based on combining ASEAN's existing FTAs and will directly compete with the TPP. . . . [I]t will sustain our regional identity and sovereignty at a time when the United States is trying to reclaim dominance in the region." China's strengthening FTA agenda appears to be its clearest response so far to the TPP (Yuan 2012).

Among China's FTA aspirations is a trilateral deal with Japan and South Korea. The prospective advantages of integrating the three economies, whose combined gross domestic product (GDP) amounts to 70 percent of East Asia's GDP and 20 percent of the world's, are important enough to Beijing to balance the defensive concerns of the Chinese automobile sector. A trilateral agreement could reverse the declining share of trade that Japan and South Korea represent for China (see Table 1.1), and enable China to advance a much-needed improvement of political relations with the two.

Japan's conservative government views China's trilateral proposal with mild interest compared to the TPP, and Chinese strategists worry that Japan's accession to the latter could diminish its interest further. The TPP would enable Japan to compete with China more effectively in US markets, leading Guoyou Song and Wen Jin Yuan to observe that from Beijing's perspective, "Japan's joining makes the TPP even more dangerous for China's economic interests" (2012: 210). While China broadens its FTA agenda to hedge against the TPP, Japan appears to be supporting the TPP to hedge against China's growing regional influence. Simultaneously pursuing the trilateral deal with China and the TPP is a logical course for Japan, whose dual strategy of "hedging and engagement" is becoming a regional phenomenon. Australia, another TPP member, has shown that a bilateral FTA with China leaves the door open to the rising tide of Chinese investment (especially in agriculture and infrastructure) despite TPP restrictions on SOEs and government finance (see Chapter 10).

Like Japan, several Latin American nations see benefits in concurrent partnerships with the United States and China. For these nations, the dangers of overreliance on the former, and benefits of deeper integration with the latter, became evident during global financial crisis. Diminishing exports to the United States were offset by Chinese demand for energy and minerals, though the "resource boom" did little for Mexico and others whose economies are oriented to manufacturing. The four members of the Pacific Alliance (PA)—Mexico, Peru, Colombia, and Chile—have articulated their common interest in more extensive engagement with China and other Asian economies, and to this end they are working to harmonize their own trade and investment regulations.

China has been a top economic partner for the PA and TPP nations (see Figure 1.1) and a major investor in Peru in particular. The four nevertheless maintain parallel trade pacts with their traditional partners, including bilateral FTAs with the United States and the European Union. In July 2013 the US government indicated its support for the initiative by becoming an observer. As members of APEC, three of the four—Chile, Mexico, and Peru—are also party to the TPP negotiations. Costa Rica's trade minister has called the Pacific Alliance a "stepping stone" for small countries such

Table 1.1 China's Trade with Japan and South Korea, 2005–2014 ($ billions)

	2005	2006	2007	2008	2009	2010	2011	2012	2013	2014
Total trade	1,422	1,760	2,176	2,563	2,207	2,974	3,642	3,867	4,159	4,300
Trade with Japan	184	207	236	267	229	298	343	329	312	312
Trade with South Korea	112	134	160	186	156	207	246	256	274	290
Japan and South Korea as % of total trade	20.84	19.40	18.21	17.67	17.45	16.98	16.16	15.15	14.10	14.01

Source: UN Comtrade 2016.

Figure 1.1 TPP Members' Trade with China as Percentage of Total Trade, 2014

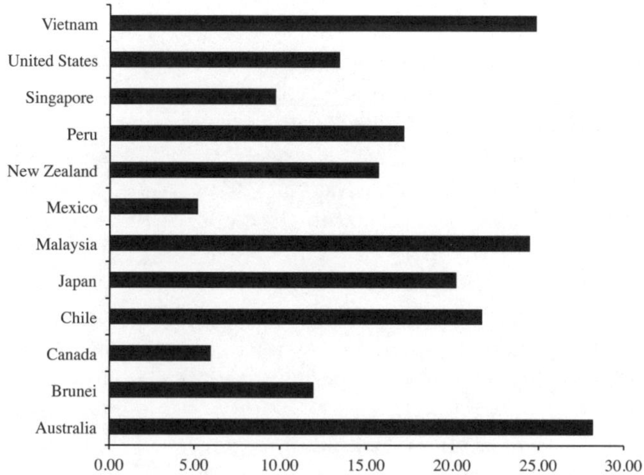

Source: UN Comtrade 2016.

as Costa Rica and Panama, which are currently candidates for PA membership, to eventually join the TPP. As argued in Chapter 4, second-tier initiatives like the PA help to prepare the way for broader "mega" deals, including the TPP and the Transatlantic Trade and Investment Partnership (TTIP).

By comparison to the PA, the TPP has generated much greater controversy in US politics. The Obama administration characterizes the TPP as an effort to raise the standards of trade and investment among member nations, but even typically pro-trade Republicans have been reluctant to support an Obama-led initiative. Meanwhile, Democratic lawmakers and activists argue that the TPP will hurt American workers, weaken food safety and financial regulations, and undermine environmental and labor standards (Lim, Elms, and Low 2012). Among the TPP's most vocal opponents is Democratic senator Elizabeth Warren, who believes that the US government's decision "to sign trade pacts and tax deals that let subsidized manufacturers around the globe sell here in America while good American jobs get shipped overseas" has "left America's middle class in a deep hole" (quoted in Goldfarb 2015).

China analyst Gordon Chang (2015) argues that US failure to advance the TPP at this stage could deal a remarkable blow not only to the US-backed global trade agenda, but also to US foreign policy in Asia. Whether intentionally or not, the TPP has become a feature of US "rebalancing" and has therefore attained a degree of strategic importance not normally attributed to trade agreements. US credibility in Asia and the relevance of the US-led trade architecture is largely staked on the success or failure of the TPP, and yet US ratification of the deal is far from certain.

President Obama's request to Congress in June 2015 to grant him trade-promotion authority, or the power to negotiate trade agreements and speed them through Congress with a yay or nay vote, was a litmus test of US resolve to advance the TPP. The House and Senate narrowly approved the authority, enabling the president to proceed with TPP negotiations and to reach an agreement with the eleven other TPP members in October 2015.

The public release of the TPP text in December 2015 did not placate its opponents. The deal's treatment of data-exclusivity for pharmaceuticals, exclusion of tobacco from investor-state dispute settlement, and perceived failure to address currency manipulation are especially controversial elements for US lawmakers. Senators Orrin Hatch, Sherrod Brown, and Lindsey Graham have cited these and other points to argue against it. Lori Wallach of Public Citizen's Global Trade Watch has characterized the TPP as "basically a Trojan horse for every kind of extreme corporate proposal that could not get passed in the sunshine of public debate" (quoted in Hirschfeld Davis 2015).

The United States and other TPP members have until February 2018 to ratify the agreement. Little opposition is expected among the TPP's Latin American members, but ratification in Malaysia and Australia could prove challenging. The Obama administration, according to *Politico* and other domestic news sources, faces an uphill battle as US trade agreements have historically required at lease two presidential terms to achieve ratification.

required at least two presidential terms to achieve ratification. Neither window is especially promising, however, as US trade agreements have historically required at least two presidential terms to achieve ratification.

As the US domestic debate rages, the other eleven TPP countries are acutely aware that without US support the deal is unlikely to progress. At least six signatories—comprising 85 percent of the TPP's total GDP—must ratify it to ensure implementation. This will require ratification by the United States and Japan, which together account for more than two-thirds of the TPP's total GDP (see Figure 1.2).

If the TPP eventually comes into force, the uncertainties will only multiply as the signatories roll out unprecedented new governance frameworks for business, government, and society. The uncertainties extend to China, where perspectives of the TPP are also in flux. The criticisms voiced above by Chinese analysts contrast with their foreign ministry's reaction when the TPP was signed in October 2015: "China is open to any mechanism that follows rules of the World Trade Organization and can boost the economic integration of the Asia-Pacific. . . . China hopes the TPP pact and other free trade arrangements in the region can boost each

Figure 1.2 Members' Share of Overall TPP Gross Domestic Product, 2014

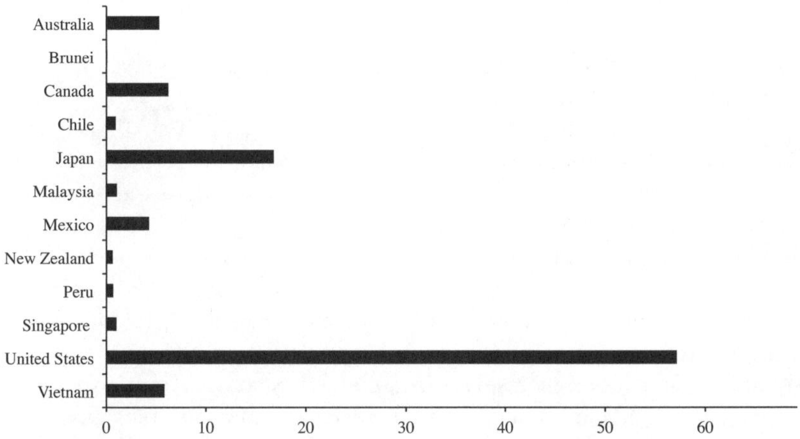

Source: World Bank 2014.

other and contribute to the Asia-Pacific's trade, investment and economic growth" (*Xinhua News* 2015).

The Chinese government has periodically signaled that eventually it may consider joining the TPP (Hearn 2013b). Several of the book's contributors find that this position aligns with the government's plan to deepen domestic economic reforms. China's reformers are advocating controversial propositions such as the expansion of the Shanghai Free Trade Zone and bilateral investment treaties with the United States and the European Union, and they believe the TPP could create an economic environment conducive to these goals. But powerful domestic interest groups, including the heavily subsidized automobile industry, oppose further liberalization of the Chinese economy. Which party prevails in this argument, and how comprehensively it does so, will condition China's relationship with the TPP and in turn propel the region either toward integration or disintegration.

Outline of the Book

The volume assesses the prospects for Asia Pacific integration at a time when new approaches to multilateral cooperation, and the domestic reforms it demands, are reformulating the regional landscape. The project originated in a workshop titled "China, Latin America, and the Changing Architecture of Trans-Pacific Engagement," cohosted in Washington, D.C., in May 2013 by the Latin American Studies Association (LASA) Section for Asia and the Americas and the Inter-American Dialogue's China and Latin America program. Funded by the Open Society Foundations and the Worldwide Universities Network, that exchange of ideas inspired the book's convocation of ten experts with diverse disciplinary backgrounds, professional affiliations, and personal perspectives.

For the three nations that are party to both the Pacific Alliance and the Transpacific Partnership (Chile, Mexico, and Peru), the former is viewed as a preparatory step for the latter, which may eventually attract other Latin American members. Ariel Armony, Nashira Chávez, and Adrian Hearn find in Chapter 2 that diplomats, policy advisers, and scholars interviewed in these three countries aspire to capitalize particularly on China's growing significance for Latin America, albeit with distinct domestic agendas. The PA countries have always *faced* West, but only recently have they *looked* West and envisioned themselves as a collective coastal frontier or "Pacific Corridor" to channel intensifying transpacific trade and investment. While the PA's embrace of market liberalization resonates with the (abandoned) US proposal to establish a Free Trade Area of the Americas (FTAA), the chapter notes Chilean president Michelle Bachelet's simultaneous commitment to deepening relations with the more state-oriented Mercosur (Southern Common Market) bloc. The resulting ideological tensions, the authors find, reflect a broader regional debate about the international leadership credentials of the United States.

US preeminence is also on the minds of Chinese strategists, particularly as the TPP sets out to liberalize the rules of East Asian integration. Jianmin Jin argues in Chapter 3 that the TPP forces a choice upon Beijing: join a US-led initiative or risk being excluded from a process that may shape the region's future economic trajectory. Jin finds that the prior option is less problematic than it may seem, as the TPP coincides to an extent with the Xi administration's efforts to introduce market reforms into the Chinese economy. These efforts are evident in the Shanghai Free Trade Zone, the State Council's announcement that a negative list will be applied to foreign investors in China's health services sector, and nascent Chinese investment agreements with the United States and the European Union. The TPP therefore constitutes an external justification for the government to carry out its domestic reform agenda. The endgame for Beijing is a robust domestic economy that underpins a regional leadership position capable of withstanding prospective foreign challenges. Jin notes the resulting paradox: cooperating with the United States over the long term will reduce the capacity of a US-led alliance to contain China.

If the TPP comes into force its proponents will gradually seek to expand its membership, which at present is limited to APEC nations. To this end, the Pacific Alliance may serve as a conduit for new Latin American members, particularly if the objectives of the two initiatives continue to align. As well as TPP members Chile, Mexico, and Peru, the PA also includes Colombia (and prospectively Costa Rica), countries that are seeking entry to APEC and that may eventually be admitted to the TPP if they adopt the required regulatory reforms. Chapter 4 by Barbara Kotschwar explores this prospect, noting that a parallel process is under way in East Asia, driven by China's regional ambitions. ASEAN has ten core members (four of which are included in the TPP) and has established FTAs with its six main trade partners. With Chinese support, ASEAN has proposed to unify the region's fragmented institutional landscape through RCEP, which as noted earlier has the capacity to compete with the TPP. And yet, Kotschwar argues, RCEP and the TPP harbor enough similarities to come together in support of APEC's long-standing ambition to create a Free Trade Area of the Asia Pacific (FTAAP).

The TPP and RCEP both seek to liberalize trade and investment, but they approach this goal from different orientations. The former seeks strict adherence to provisions on state-owned enterprises, intellectual property, and investor-state dispute settlement, while the latter permits its members flexibility in setting the timeframe and scope of reforms. RCEP's ASEAN-style "consensus" approach augments its appeal for some members, but as Zhang Xuegang argues in Chapter 5, resulting exemptions and exceptions also weaken its cohesion. Zhang finds that RCEP poses three main challenges for China: (1) to open its agriculture, finance, and energy sectors to external competition at a time when domestic sectoral interest groups are gaining political influence; (2) to rapidly establish bilateral FTAs (particularly with Japan, South Korea, and India) that would formulate detailed country-level strategies and thus prepare the way for RCEP; and (3) to support RCEP as an alternative to the TPP while simultaneously deepening economic integration with the United States. These challenges, Zhang argues, are integral to President Xi's proposed "new type of great power relations."

The TPP has accelerated China's pursuit of alternative multilateral agreements that might diminish the TPP's influence, but the Chinese Ministries of Commerce and Foreign Affairs have also signaled that their government has an "open mind" about joining the TPP. Tim Summers argues in Chapter 6 that these seemingly diverging signals reflect China's post–Cold War strategy of simultaneous "engagement" and "diversification." This is evident in Beijing's "turn to multilateralism" through accession to APEC, ASEAN, and the ASEAN Regional Forum (ARF) on the one hand, and concurrent openness to new bilateral FTAs and institutions like RCEP (and ostensibly the TPP) on the other. The former trend engages China in an expanding network of trade and cooperation agreements, while the latter diversifies the regional institutional landscape in order to dilute the impact of potentially hostile alliances. The goal of China's dual strategy,

Summers concludes, is to see the TPP become "one more noodle in the bowl."

In contrast to US foreign investment policies, Chinese president Xi has contended that the free movement of finance across borders undermines economic stability in the developing world. Kevin Gallagher argues in Chapter 7 that to stabilize twenty-first-century trade and investment, the TPP must widen rather than diminish the ability of signatories to regulate the inflow and outflow of capital and to restructure their sovereign debts. Gallagher's textual dissection of the US-Peru Trade Treaty and the US Model Bilateral Investment Treaty leads him to argue that the TPP offers an opportunity to improve on past practice. This position is supported by the International Monetary Fund's recent warning about the "limited flexibility" of emerging trade and investment agreements. US negotiators eventually conceded more flexibility on financial regulation in the TPP, but only after Chile, Malaysia, and progressive members of the US Congress threatened to otherwise withdraw support. The lesson to be drawn, writes Gallagher, is that regional integration under the TPP (or any other model) will attract greater support when governments are afforded the legal ability to protect their financial systems from capital flight.

While the flow of finance across borders stirs diplomatic tensions, the flow of food provokes controversy across government, business, and society. Agriculture disputes precipitated the demise of the World Trade Organization (WTO) Doha round, and as Alan Smart and Josephine Smart write in Chapter 8, "agricultural exceptionalism" now jeopardizes the TPP. The proposed tariff reductions favor large export-oriented agribusiness, but pose challenges for small farmers unable to compete with international economies of scale. Furthermore, conflicts between producers and consumers over the health and safety risks of mass production—and how these risks are scientifically assessed—echo disputes since the 1980s about the institutional causes of mad cow disease and foot and mouth disease. The TPP's critics argue that the agreement will magnify these risks by insisting that food products are safe unless scientifically proven otherwise, and by undermining the livelihoods of small farmers and the well-being of consumers. According to the chapter's authors, the new politics of food safety, combined with the old politics of agricultural protection, constitutes a minefield of political risk standing in the path of reform. Investments from Chinese state enterprises in the agriculture sectors of TPP members Australia, Canada, and the United States add heat to the debate as regulators wrestle with the encroachment of foreign SOEs on national land and concerns about the safety of their large-scale operations.

Whether or not Chinese SOEs prioritize political interests over profitability in their overseas operations is debatable. More certain is that existing regulatory frameworks are better equipped to govern investment from private than government sources, and that the TPP seeks to redress this regulatory gap. Chapter 9 by Adrian Hearn examines Chinese outbound agriculture investment, finding that similar reactions, including allegations of tax avoidance and land grabs, have emerged in contexts as diverse as Australia and Brazil. While the TPP may enable Australia to limit the activities of national and foreign SOEs within its borders, Hearn argues that Chinese investors and their foreign partners have at their disposal countermeasures to circumvent any such restrictions. These include bilateral FTAs that carve out exceptions to the TPP (such as the China-Australia FTA), acquisition of large multinational private firms (such as Noble Group and Nidera in 2014), and empowerment of the Chinese private sector to conduct overseas deals. In light of these countermeasures, the chapter concludes that the TPP should aim less to limit the capacities of SOEs than to encourage foreign investment—whether public or private—that expands value-adding segments of agriculture production chains.

The final chapter, by Adrian Hearn and Margaret Myers, draws together the book's contents, noting that sophisticated diplomacy is becoming more necessary as governments try to balance the opportunities created by China's rise, with participation in emerging international frameworks of trade and investment. The ideological and practical dilemmas of this balance are forcing Asia Pacific nations to consider how closer integration with China may or may not coexist with market-oriented multilateralism. The resulting challenge they face is to formulate strategies that leverage simultaneous benefits from the distinct models of governance that are vying for regional preeminence.

The chapters invite reflection on the changing currents of transpacific integration at a critical moment in Asia Pacific history. The Eastward shift of global economic dynamism brings with it new competitive tensions and cooperative opportunities underpinned by different visions of regionalism. Whether these visions are flexible enough to avert antagonism or too rigid to accommodate each other will determine the meaning of "Asia Pacific" in the twenty-first century. How the emerging "mega-region" is defined will ultimately provide an answer to the encompassing question: Is the Asia Pacific on the cusp of integration or disintegration?

2

Latin American Visions of Transpacific Integration

Ariel C. Armony, Nashira P. Chávez, and Adrian H. Hearn

THE PACIFIC ALLIANCE (PA) AND THE TRANS-PACIFIC PARTNERSHIP (TPP) represent the onset of new regional practices in response to twenty-first-century globalization, marked by accelerated change in the international system. They transcend traditional notions of regional space and interconnection in order to create strategically integrated blocs for the evolving international environment. Their nature and parameters are based in the open economic order that has proliferated since the 1980s, yet they bypass the creation of multinational blocs defined in terms of their geographic proximity. For Latin America, both initiatives represent collective efforts to overcome the disadvantages of small economies in relation to recent economic trends in Asia. They are, in sum, complex transregional endeavors driven by a new approach to policy coordination and recognition of the Asia Pacific region's growing economic dynamism.

This chapter explores Latin American perspectives of the PA and TPP in relation to twenty-first-century regionalism. It concentrates on three nations that are party to both initiatives—Chile, Mexico, and Peru—to examine how domestic policy orientations are influenced by regional dynamics, perceptions of state-market interactions, and faith in the international leadership capacity of the United States. Data drawn from interviews with key players in these three nations illuminate the motivations guiding their engagement with the two initiatives.

The PA and TPP seek to coordinate policies in response to the accelerated growth of emerging markets. The three nations under discussion are attempting to build interstate cooperation stimulated by their shared perception of the Asia Pacific region as the next economic frontier. To explore this perception, between 2013 and 2015 we interviewed a series of professionals with authoritative knowledge of their nations' Asia Pacific relations. With backgrounds spanning policymaking to academia, our interviewees included diplomatic officials, free trade negotiators, former ministers of economics and foreign trade, and scholars. We asked between three and four respondents for each country a set of thirteen questions with the intent to standardize data collection and compare answers within and between countries. Interviews were conducted in Spanish via telephone or voice communication sessions over the Internet, ranging from forty-five to ninety minutes. Through these discussions we tried to discern the interest of the three nations in the PA and TPP, identify the themes that respondents viewed as most important, and illuminate the interpretative factors that inform domestic debates on the two initiatives.

Viewpoints of former and current government officials are important because these individuals constitute an epistemic community, namely "a network of professionals with recognized expertise and competence in a particular domain or issue area" (Haas 1992: 3). Research in global governance and regionalism provides strong evidence of the ability of such knowledge-based actors and networks to have a high degree of influence on policy outcomes (Cross 2013). Powerful state and nonstate actors rely on their expertise to construct rules and norms. The perceptions of other societal actors—particularly those representing subaltern groups—are also important, but neither the PA nor the TPP has so far significantly accommodated bottom-up concerns at the negotiating table.

In a context of uncertainty about both initiatives, perceptions expressed by epistemic communities shed light on potential policy directions. As noted, to standardize our data we employed a structured comparative method, which solicited each of our interviewees to respond to the same questions. Their answers revealed a set of beliefs about the roles of Chile, Mexico, and Peru in new regionalisms; the parameters defining national goals; social-institutional idiosyncrasies; and the material constraints conditioning these phenomena. Understanding these beliefs is important in the early stages of policymaking, particularly considering the uncharted nature of emerging transpacific connections.

Globalization's Next Big Thing

The Economist recently described the Pacific Alliance as a "brilliant piece of diplomatic marketing," but also noted that "now it has to add substance" (2013: 38). The bloc's purpose has indeed been well staged in international media, but it is not yet possible to assess its practical significance. Since its inception in 2012, the PA has advanced toward the harmonization of its members' intratrade and financial agreements (agreeing in 2014 to liberalize 92 percent of internal trade), the movement of people between them, and the establishment of common platforms for their trade promotion agencies. The bloc's "diplomatic marketing" has clearly spearheaded this evolution, evident since its first business summit in 2013, which brought together the members' heads of state in the context of the United Nations General Assembly. Expositions promoting the PA's economic potentials have taken place in London, Tokyo, Delhi, Moscow, Madrid, and Taiwan, as well as at the Davos Economic Forum.

The TPP is also a work in progress. Having signed off on the final text in October 2015, the twelve member governments now face the challenges of ratifying the agreement and positioning themselves to implement it. Defined by the United States as "a landmark, 21st-century trade agreement," the TPP attempts to advance a new template of rules and provisions for the exchange of goods and services (USTR 2015). Public information on the policy positions of TPP nations regarding intellectual property, rules of origin, environmental standards, and other key points was scant during the negotiations. This generated concerns from civil society organizations in TPP countries, which seized on leaked documents to criticize the secrecy and nondemocratic process characterizing the endeavor.

The TPP's future will depend largely on domestic developments in the United States, which joined the initiative in 2009 and has since been seen as its leader because of the critical market and source of investment it represents for all negotiating countries. The United States is also the member with the most assertive agenda, and the main proponent of strategies for balancing China's growing influence in Asia and the world. But support for the TPP is tentative even within the United States, where a deeply divisive debate preceded eventual congressional approval in 2015 for "fast-track" trade-promotion authority to negotiate the TPP without further public deliberation. Any further legal setbacks or delays may prompt TPP nations to lose confidence in the capacity of US negotiators to follow through with their commitments.

As the PA and TPP negotiations advance, diplomats, trade representatives, and public commentators are influencing domestic debates about their risks and benefits. The voices of these "epistemic communities" provide insights into national and subnational perspectives on how individual countries should participate in new multilateral structures of transpacific engagement. As discussed later, for Chile, Mexico, and Peru this process raises a question of historic magnitude: how to balance long-standing dependence on the United States with the opportunities generated by the emergence of Asia.

The PA and TPP have emerged in the context of uneven globalization, the proliferation of economic crises in industrialized countries, and the growing importance of developing economies. The roots of these processes can be traced to the post–World War II open international system advanced by the United States to stabilize the global order through free trade, capital accumulation, and investment (Kindleberger 1973). The long-term trend has been toward interdependence through accelerated international cooperation between states and the integration of their markets. This interdependence has proceeded unevenly, producing fractioned economic trajectories at the global, regional, national, and subnational levels. Today the ratio of the average income between the richest and poorest country is sixty to one, compared to nine to one in the nineteenth century (Birdsall 2002).

Mainstream development studies claim that the widening gap between rich and poor nations is not the result of globalization. Rather, globalization is argued to have mitigated inequality among nations that adopt policies of economic liberalization and free trade (Lindert and Williamson 2003). Such policies ostensibly advance income convergence among participants in the global market, with China and India serving as two recent examples. Rooted in this economic philosophy, the PA and TPP are promoted by their proponents as potential mechanisms to reduce income asymmetries and poverty.

The creation of transpacific trade and investment blocs reflects a shift of economic dynamism to emerging nations, which contributed 60 percent of global growth between 2006 and 2010 alone (World Economic Forum 2013b). The BRIC countries (Brazil, Russia, India, and China) in particular outperformed until recently, thanks to high commodity prices, low inflation, and stable macroeconomic policies (Patterson 2013). Despite recent indications of slower growth among these countries, by 2030 the economies of China, Russia, Brazil, and India are projected to surpass those of the Group of Seven (G7). Their rapid urbanization and growing middle classes (expected to reach 1.8 billion people by 2020) imply massive infrastructure development and demand for value-added products and services (Wilson, Kelston, and Ahmed 2010).

Emerging economies currently represent 26 percent of the global economy, and market indexes continue to project their long-term growth. The 2005 prediction of Goldman Sachs that the next eleven countries to exert a transformative global impact would be "emerging" has largely proved accurate (O'Neill et al. 2005). Coined the Next 11 (N-11), Vietnam, Bangladesh, Pakistan, Indonesia, Mexico, South Korea, the Philippines, Turkey, Iran, Egypt, and Nigeria exhibit similar patterns of economic growth, urbanization, and development of human capital, connectivity, and infrastructure as the BRICs (Lawson, Heacock, and Stupnystka 2007). Six of these nations are in Asia, and their relative rise to prominence has been underpinned by the international financial crisis that began in 2008–2009, generating the first global recession since World War II. The US housing bubble, liquidity crisis, and national debt, accompanied by China's international expansion, have set in motion a gradual destabilization of North-South economic structures and an associated ascendance of South-South (particularly South-East) alternatives.

Despite the mounting problems of neoliberal interdependence, developing countries have largely managed to return to their previous growth trajectories. They have consequently argued for more authority in the International Monetary Fund (IMF) and other global economic institutions. The formal replacement of the G7 by the Group of 20 (G20) in 2008 as the preeminent multilateral venue for setting the global economic policy agenda, and the announcement of the New Development Bank at the 2014 BRICS summit in Brazil, are emblematic of this shift. At its core lies an impressive set of figures: emerging economies now hold almost two-thirds of global reserves, and as foreign investment flows into them like never before, they are expected to account for 60 percent of the world's gross domestic product (GDP) by 2030 (OECD 2013). This new global economic environment is the fundamental stimulus behind the PA and TPP.

Old and New Regionalisms

The interest of Chile, Mexico, and Peru in the Pacific Alliance and the Trans-Pacific Partnership reflects their endorsement of the realist-institutionalist model of international organization that has prevailed for the past five decades, in which market-friendly states are the main actors. Advancing this model, the PA and TPP negotiations have largely been driven from the top down, with civil society voices marginal to the process. There is no formal mechanism for incorporating independent voices into the PA deliberations, which have been conducted exclusively among business and political elites. The TPP summits were somewhat more inclusive, providing independent interest groups a "room next door" to advocate their concerns to negotiators. However, the attentiveness (and attendance) of negotiators to these briefing sessions was voluntary. The lack of vertical state-society engagement in the TPP process gave rise to widespread criticism that it amounted to a series of "secret" negotiations (Amnesty International 2012).

The PA and TPP harbor a legacy of expectations about the potentials and limits of multilateralism. The World Trade Organization (WTO) and other late-twentieth-century pacts such as the Asia Pacific Economic Cooperation (APEC) forum, the North American Free Trade Agreement (NAFTA), and the Southern Common Market (Mercosur) have each generated broad familiarity with multilateral architectures of integration. The breakdown of the WTO's Doha-round negotiations has nevertheless revealed entrenched obstacles in the multilateral process and stimulated a worldwide pursuit of bilateral free trade agreements. The PA and TPP project a flexible vision of multilateralism, advancing a collective agenda of liberalization among "like-minded" governments while affording members the freedom to engage in other parallel agreements. As Zhang Xuegang notes in Chapter 5, the TPP explicitly sets "high standards" of liberalization as a condition of entry in order to transcend and circumvent the detailed debates that have bogged down the WTO Doha round.

Geographic considerations naturally continue to condition Chilean, Mexican, and Peruvian perspectives, though in a less constrictive fashion than has previously been the case. The three nations have always *faced* West from the shores of the Pacific, but only recently have they begun to *look* West and formulate their orientation in terms of a "Pacific Corridor" and "Pacific Alliance." This orientation sets its sights beyond the traditional sphere of regional interaction, seeking distinctive partnerships that accommodate the accumulation of global capital in Asia's emerging markets. It is a strategy clearly articulated in the PA's official statements and confirmed in the confidential interviews conducted for this chapter as an attempt to "design a strategy towards the diversification of economic and financial relations between Latin America and Asia," according to one of the Mexican interviewees. The PA and TPP are thus viewed as complementary, representing an opportunity to affirm Latin America's integration with the "Pacific Arc" through a pragmatic commitment to the free movement of goods, services, and capital.

With trade and investment facilitation as core goals, the PA is first and foremost an economic initiative, with diplomatic considerations and the prospect of political union taking a distant second place. Advancements on the creation of a platform for promoting academic mobility and talk of an interparliamentary body to enforce compliance with regional accords are securely couched in economic rationale. In this respect the PA (and the TPP) transcend many of the political complexities that characterize the European Union. Beyond the TPP's push for independent investor-state dispute settlement, there are no aspirations for supranational regulatory entities. Their economic focus reflects both initiatives' attempt to foment cooperation between nations in Asia and the Americas, whose geographic dispersion diminishes the potential for more direct physical linkages.

Bringing together its members' existing bilateral and multilateral free trade agreements (see Table 2.1), the PA raises the prospect of a cross-national supply chain, shared production costs, economies of scale, and a platform for collectively adding value. The Chilean, Mexican, and Peruvian specialists interviewed for this chapter perceived the TPP as a natural amplifier of the PA's ambitions, albeit a less endogenous one. They expressed pride that the PA is Latin American in origin, while the TPP has evolved from the dominance of the United States in global economic affairs. The two agreements are viewed as complementary and mutually reinforcing, but not inherently intertwined.

The four countries of the Pacific Alliance together constitute the sixth largest economy in the world and the seventh largest recipient of foreign

Table 2.1 Chile, Mexico, and Peru: Trade Agreements in Force

	Chile	Mexico	Peru
North America	Canada, Mexico, United States	Canada, United States	Canada, Mexico, United States
Central America	Costa Rica, El Salvador, Guatemala, Honduras, Panama	Costa Rica, El Salvador, Guatemala, Honduras, Nicaragua, Panama	Costa Rica, Guatemala, Panama
South America	Argentina, Bolivia, Colombia, Ecuador, Peru, Venezuela, Mercosur	Argentina, Bolivia, Brazil, Chile, Colombia, Ecuador, Paraguay, Peru, Uruguay, Mercosur	Bolivia, Chile, Colombia, Ecuador, Venezuela, Mercosur
Asia	Brunei, China, India, Japan, Malaysia, Republic of Korea, Singapore, Thailand, Vietnam	Japan	China, Japan, Singapore, South Korea, Thailand
Oceania	Australia, New Zealand		
Europe	European Free Trade Association, European Union, Turkey	European Free Trade Association, European Union	European Free Trade Association, European Union
Middle East		Israel	

Source: Organization of American States.

direct investment, with a 4.5 percent share of global foreign direct investment (FDI). Within Latin America, the PA countries represent 50 percent of total trade and 35 percent of total GDP. Their aggregate unemployment rate is 6.5 percent and their average inflation is 3.7 percent, below the regional average of 4.6 percent (Table 2.2 shows the disaggregated indicators). They have achieved average growth of 2.7 percent, which is higher than average for Latin America (1.4 percent), the United States (2.4 percent), Europe (1.4 percent), and the world (2.5 percent). The PA's attempt to forge closer integration with the developing economies of Asia (which have consistently achieved growth exceeding 7 percent) adds currency to the above projections about the global South as the future engine of the world economy.

The TPP is a more complex endeavor than the PA. More than twenty rounds of TPP negotiations grappled with members' differences over e-commerce, environment, customs, intellectual property, labor, telecommunications, and investor-state dispute settlement. It is an ostensibly "high-standard" model agreement for twenty-first-century trade and investment that seeks to foment closer integration among its members in commercial pursuits as well as in research, technological upgrading, and education. The TPP's Western Hemisphere members are already linked to each other through bilateral free trade agreements (FTAs), giving them a strong basis for collectively engaging with Asia. Indeed, for Latin America's TPP members the agreement's cornerstone is the creation of a pathway for dealing with Asia on more favorable terms than have so far been the case. Should the TPP expand to include Indonesia, Laos, the Philippines, and Thailand alongside current members Brunei, Japan, Malaysia, Singapore, and Vietnam, Latin America's participants will gain access to a region responsible

Table 2.2 Chile, Mexico, and Peru's Economies in Context, 2014

	Chile	Mexico	Peru
GDP (current $ billions)	258	1,295	203
GDP growth (annual percentage)	1.9	2.2	2.4
GDP per capita (current $)	14,528	10,326	6,541
Trade (percentage of GDP)	66.1	65.9	43.6
Inflation (percentage)	5.4	4.7	3.0
Foreign direct investment, net inflows (balance of payments, current $ billions)	22	24	7.8
Logistics performance index: quality of trade and transport-related infrastructure (1 = low to 5 = high)	3.2	3.0	2.7

Source: World Bank, World Development Indicators.

Figure 2.1 Chile's Main Partners (Exports), 2015

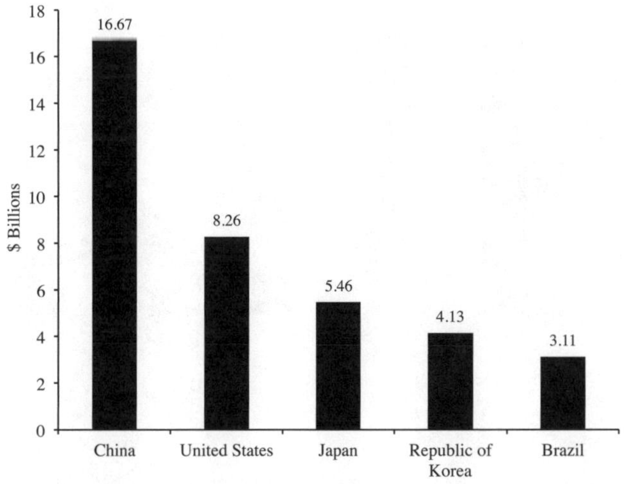

Source: UN Comtrade 2016.

Figure 2.2 Mexico's Main Partners (Exports), 2014

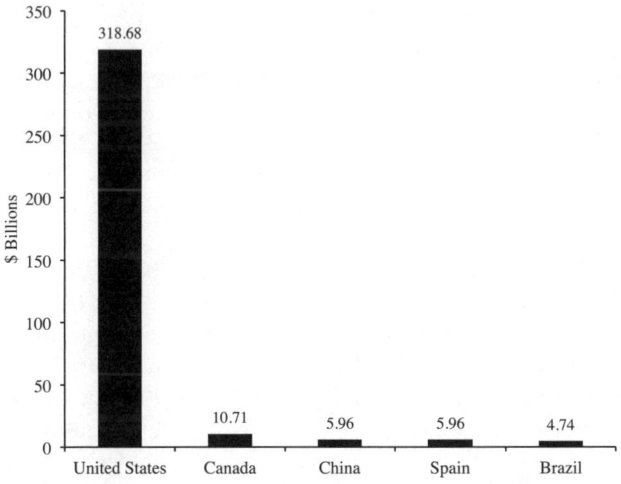

Source: UN Comtrade 2016.

Figure 2.3 Peru's Main Partners (Exports), 2014

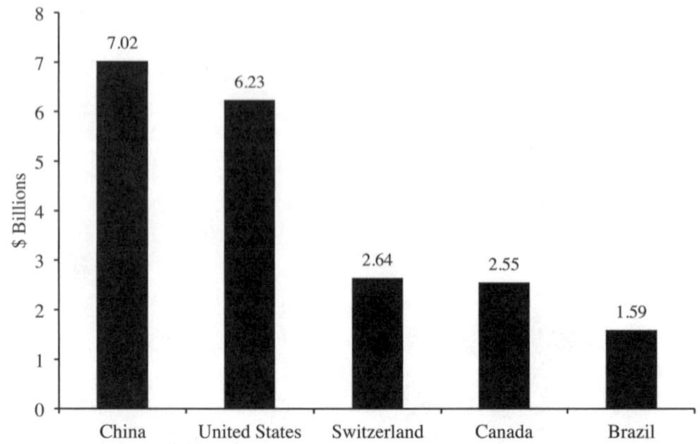

Source: UN Comtrade 2016.

for 40 percent of global trade. Figures 2.1, 2.2, and 2.3 illustrate the current main trading partners (in terms of exports) for Chile, Mexico, and Peru.

Citing their nations' trade indicators, interviewees in Chile and Peru viewed the TPP as a choice rather than an imperative. By 2015, 43 percent of Chile's and by 2014 27 percent of Peru's exports went to ASEAN+3 (Association of Southeast Asian Nations). Given that both nations already have bilateral agreements with China, Japan, and South Korea, the TPP does not expose them to new trade risks. By contrast, Mexico's similar production structure to many Asian countries and its attempt to maintain ground in the NAFTA market with the United States and Canada (both TPP members) have bred a cautious approach to the Pacific region. Mexico sent less than 3 percent of its total exports to ASEAN+3 in 2014, and its only Asian FTA is with Japan. The Mexican government nevertheless views the value chain integration afforded by the TPP (and PA) as a vehicle to mitigate its market disadvantages.

Interviewees in the three countries shared the belief that the TPP could enable them to harmonize their various bilateral accords, refine the FTAs that each holds with the United States, and provide a platform for future agreements in the Pacific region, especially with Southeast Asia. According to a Chilean respondent, "regional templates with a vast number of partners tend to harmonize chapters; they do not overturn bilateral agreements. . . . [E]conomic actors will decide which agreement suits them better." Like the PA, the TPP was thus described as a starting point for a new kind of regionalism that could draw on economic dynamism in Asia to the advantage of Latin America.

Diverging Ideologies of Regionalism

Despite doubts about the eventual consistency of the PA and quality of the TPP framework, interviewees in the three countries were generally enthusiastic about both. This positive outlook is premised on an instrumental calculus that yields access to Asia's rapidly growing markets and generates absolute economic gains. As one respondent put it: "We believe these agreements should be 'trade-creating' rather than 'trade-diverting.' Thus our search for multiple agreements is a priority in order to minimize trade costs. We believe that relying on a small number of partners distorts trade; since we need to expand trade the TPP is attractive. It may be the starting point for a larger agreement with the Pacific Corridor."

Former Colombian trade minister Sergio Díaz-Granados has stated that the PA "is an important signal to Latin America, in the sense that regional integration and open markets are the best way to ensure a greater volume of investment, trade, and growth" (quoted in Dube 2013). It remains to be seen how effectively this signal will stimulate cooperation with the comparatively less market-oriented visions of Latin American regionalism espoused by Mercosur, the Union of South American Nations (Unasur), and the Bolivarian Alliance for the Peoples of Our America (ALBA). President Juan Manuel Santos of Colombia has argued that the PA is an economic hub that is not intended to generate friction with other regional initiatives. Nevertheless, the fracture and contrast with these other Latin American projects is clear. The PA is to some degree a response to the mixed results of Mercosur's internal tensions over the membership of Venezuela, the temporary suspension of Paraguay from the bloc following the impeachment of President Fernando Lugo, and the trade disputes and barriers between its leading actors, Brazil and Argentina.

Subdued economic performance in Mercosur coincides with the bloc's imposition of a 35 percent common external tariff on imports since 2012, and it stands in contrast to the positive trade and investment profile registered over the same period by the PA nations. A similar contrast is evident when comparing the PA to the Community of Andean Nations (CAN), which despite being one of the oldest regional projects has not been able to advance a collective economic agenda. This is evident in the decision of two key CAN members, Peru and Colombia, to establish unilateral trade agreements with the European Union. The prospects for establishing a more profound integration between Mercosur and CAN are far from certain, and few maintain hopes of bringing such disparate agreements as Unasur, ALBA, and the Latin American Integration Association (ALADI) into a common Latin American framework. The PA's pursuit of "competitive liberalization," oriented toward engagement with actors across the Pacific, exhibits a more flexible and potentially generalizable foundation for regionalism.

Each of the PA nations has for several decades advanced an agenda of minimal state intervention in economic affairs and more streamlined social programs and protections (Murillo, Oliveros, and Vaishnav 2011). It is no coincidence that they were the countries most supportive of the failed Free Trade Area of the Americas (FTAA), which espoused a similar political philosophy. The exception to this tendency is Chilean president Michelle Bachelet, reelected in 2014 on a center-left platform that envisions closer relations with alternative regional initiatives. Her government program indicates support for the PA, but that Chile's participation in it will not be "antagonistic with other integrational projects in the region" (quoted in *Perú 21* 2013). The same document harbors a veiled criticism of the outgoing administration of Miguel Juan Sebastián Piñera: "Chile's presence in the region has diminished, its relations with its neighbors are problematic, and a mercantilist vision of our Latin American links has been imposed." While Bachelet's social democratic vision may contrast with those prevailing in Mexico, Colombia, and Peru, the PA will in all likelihood continue to champion a free market political-economic vision.

As members of both the PA and the TPP, Chile, Mexico, and Peru perceive a natural affinity between the two agreements. Openness, attraction of foreign investment, and reduction of transaction costs underpin a common agenda of growth through trade liberalization. Animated by this agenda, the PA and TPP are viewed as vehicles to upgrade existing FTAs with the United States while speeding up expansion into such markets as Australia and New Zealand.

In Latin America's fragmented context of disparate agreements, any step toward harmonization of regional affairs harbors strong appeal. Even more than the PA, the TPP represents such a step, with the caveat that the ongoing support of its Latin American members derives largely from the extent to which it enables them to behave more freely in relation to the United States. Strong US advocacy of the TPP is perceived in economic terms, since the Pacific region represents 61 percent of US manufactured exports and 75 percent of US agricultural exports. Although US negotiators are bargaining hard to advance the interests of their nation's corporations, for instance through intellectual property and copyright provisions that could curtail access to generic pharmaceuticals, there is an expectation in Chile, Mexico, and Peru that the United States will assume a "rational and flexible" leadership role.

The degree to which US negotiators will adopt such a conciliatory approach remains to be seen, but commentators particularly in Chile and Peru perceive the TPP as an egalitarian proposition that will lead to broadly consensual outcomes. As an interviewee noted, "The fear is that the United States is attempting to advance its own agenda on topics such as intellectual property rights, among others. Yet, we believe the U.S. realizes that it needs to be flexible enough given the multiplicity of partners." As long as the United States can offer a broad framework that benefits all participants, the TPP will maintain traction among its Latin American members. The latter are optimistic in this regard, as they believe Washington must necessarily adopt a flexible stance when dealing with such a diverse group.

The long process of working toward TPP ratification is not viewed as an impediment to the PA's progress, but several of our respondents indicated that the failure of the former would be a blow to the latter. To succeed, both initiatives require confidence in the international leadership credentials of the United States, which would suffer were the TPP to break down. Such an impasse in the TPP would also cast a shadow over the PA's political-economic agenda, characterized by its members' pursuit of integration on the basis of open markets, deregulation, and state retrenchment.

Chile's long-standing enthusiasm for the TPP derives from its participation in the precursor Pacific 4 (P4) agreement with Brunei, Singapore, and New Zealand. Interviewees described the TPP as a mechanism for both countering the gridlock of the Doha round and generating the necessary momentum to revive the WTO process. Our Chilean respondents saw their country as part of the globalized developed world and were optimistic that the TPP will not raise serious competitive problems. The corollary is that neither the TPP nor the PA is expected to open new doors for Chile in strictly commercial terms. Rather, the agreements could enable Chile to more effectively organize and operationalize its existing partnerships.

Like their Chilean counterparts, our Peruvian respondents were upbeat about the competitive dynamics of the PA and TPP. They described Peru's FTA with the United States, signed in 2006, as a positive experience that allowed Peru to acquire the "know-how" to bring subsequent FTAs into effect with Singapore in 2009, China in 2010, South Korea in 2011, Thailand in 2011, and Japan in 2012. The TPP is envisioned as a platform for upgrading these agreements and attracting new investment, goals that the PA complements by facilitating closer integration particularly with Chile. The two agreements are thus seen as mutually supportive pursuits that augment Peru's leverage in the Asia Pacific region, including with Australia and New Zealand. Furthermore, improved access to Asia Pacific markets is expected to generate comparative advantages for Peru that might foment cooperation with Eastward-looking Brazilian, Bolivian, and Paraguayan enterprises.

Mexican respondents were more cautious than their PA counterparts about the implications of deeper trade with Asia. As noted, Mexican concerns stem from low levels of mutually beneficial transpacific trade and engagement, notwithstanding the growing relevance of Asian actors—China in particular—in Latin America. Interviewees nevertheless perceived the PA as a platform for projecting a confident international profile outward toward the "market of the twenty-first century" (that is, the Asia Pacific region). To achieve this goal, they acknowledged the need to strengthen Mexico's capacity to counterbalance Asia's expanding share of the US market, and believed that both the PA and TPP could help them to do so by "updating NAFTA." As Mexico's undersecretary for foreign trade, Francisco de Rosenzweig (2012), writes, the TPP is "without a doubt an opportunity for Mexico to deepen its relations with Asia-Pacific markets, and to reposition itself with the United States post-NAFTA." The industrial policies that for over three decades have deepened Mexico's economic integration with the United States often provoke debate among Mexican analysts, but to diversify the nation's trade partners is no simple matter. Mexico's strategy in the TPP is therefore to simultaneously defend its share of the US market while gradually broadening its foreign engagement. The TPP is seen as the best available tool for achieving these results, especially since Chinese competitive pressures show no sign of easing.

The China Factor

A key goal of the TPP and PA is to bring into effect a broad multilateral strategy for engaging with Asia. The two initiatives align in their attempt to formulate cross-Pacific relations—especially with China—from a collective position. Competition in the Chinese market is intense, and Latin American countries have little leverage and visibility. The creation of an integrated economic space with a defined image is viewed as an important countermeasure to this problem.

Our Chilean, Mexican, and Peruvian interviewees recognized that the vision of governance espoused by the PA and TPP is fundamentally different from China's. This is clearest in relation to democratic process, accountability of public officials, labor rights, individual liberties, and the role of the state in economic affairs. Consistent with the official discourse, several of our respondents argued that the Pacific Alliance is more than a trade agreement. It is also a political alliance based on the common principle of democratic values. In this respect, the PA and TPP exhibit an important divergence with China and other nondemocratic countries in Asia.

Having championed China's entry into the WTO, Chile was the first Latin American country to sign an FTA with Beijing and to see bilateral trade with China overtake trade with the United States (in 2007). For thirty-five years Chile has taken aggressive measures to open its economy, signing twenty-five trade agreements with sixty countries and implementing strict business requirements for large state-owned enterprises. For our Chilean respondents, the PA and TPP represent templates for harmonizing their nation's agreements with Mexico, Peru, and the Pacific region. The PA in particular is viewed a mechanism to compensate for a small population (17 million people) with improved visibility at the bargaining table. As a founding member of the P4 (predecessor of the TPP), Chile exhibits commitment and readiness to advance these treaties. It is also (with Mexico) one of Latin America's two members of the Organization for Economic Cooperation and Development (OECD), underpinning an official commitment to high standards of environmental protection, intellectual property rights, and transparency. These governance principles represent a potential point of friction with China, but as yet have not stood in the way of efforts to attract Chinese investment and boost bilateral trade. While their experience of authoritarian rule under Augusto Pinochet (1974–1990) has made Chileans sensitive to issues of human rights and democratic process, senior officials tend to view China in economic terms, relegating political concerns to second place.

For Mexico, China's rise has been a difficult story of intensifying competition in domestic and foreign markets (especially the United States) and a bilateral trade deficit that by 2014 had grown to $60 billion. Whether or not the PA and TPP would help to remedy this imbalance was a matter of contention among our Mexican respondents. Some felt that the two initiatives represent comprehensive strategies for diversifying Mexico's foreign trade, whose unequivocal orientation to the United States has precipitated a losing battle with Chinese exporters. Others felt that the PA and TPP do not sufficiently address Mexico's unique economic and trade concerns because both would ultimately involve even stronger reliance on the United States. From the latter perspective, a better strategy would be to formulate a China policy that is independent of the TPP. Such a strategy would promote a "triangular" dynamic that encourages Sino-Mexican investments and production chains that target the US market (see Dussel Peters, Hearn, and Shaiken 2013). While the Mexican interviewees identified the potential of the TPP to diversify and expand their nation's international commerce, they expressed greater concern than their Chilean and Peruvian counterparts about further tethering their economy to the United States.

Economic policy has also moved to the fore in Peru, a nation with long-standing migratory connections to China and home to Latin America's largest Chinese diaspora. With $15 billion of bilateral trade in 2014, China stands slightly behind the United States as Peru's main trade partner, and Peruvian negotiators are eager to attract Chinese investment into services and other sectors beyond natural resources. Their broader ambition is to position Peru as a hub that concentrates transpacific trade with the 10,000-mile North-South Pacific Corridor. Our Peruvian respondents cited Lima's long-standing ties with Beijing as a comparative advantage within the PA, raising Peru's prospects to lead their collective engagement with China. This optimism contrasts with the troubling realities of China's massive investments in Peru's mining sector, which have provoked organized protests, particularly among indigenous groups, over environmental and labor violations. Demands for stronger regulations and accountability requirements on Chinese-led investments are putting pressure on Peruvian policymakers to rethink the rules of economic engagement and encourage Chinese companies to enhance their community relations. The looming policy challenge is to leverage the governance provisions of the PA and TPP to achieve these outcomes without alienating Beijing.

Respondents in all three countries viewed the PA and TPP as strategies for insertion into Asian markets that "diversify political and commercial relations" while avoiding reliance on China. They concurred that the likelihood of this outcome would be enhanced by the broad range of alliances forged by both agreements, premised on "Western" values of competitive liberalization and democratic governance. Affirmation of these values was viewed as a shield against the economic, political, and cultural uncertainties brought by China.

Conclusion

In a region with no shortage of pacts and summits, the PA and TPP are attractive for their potential to offer something new. Policy innovation is a logical response to the rapidly changing dynamics of world trade, and the three Latin American nations discussed in this chapter have committed themselves at the highest political level to an innovative path. It is not clear how effectively this commitment will enable them to reconcile their particular economic priorities with their shared aspiration to build deeper ties with the Asia Pacific region. Chile and Peru's commodity-driven economies contrast with Mexico's more diverse industrial landscape, raising questions about the PA's ability to serve its members' needs equally. As noted earlier, Mexico has long pursued closer integration with the United States, and wishes to avoid any further threats to its share of the US market. Mexico's structural divergence from Chile and Peru foreshadows a series of long-term tensions and crosscutting purposes within the PA.

A further challenge facing the PA is the low level of economic interdependence between its members, which results from the incapacity of existing infrastructure to bridge the large distances within and between them. Under these conditions the PA's aspirations to liberalize trade and promote the free movement of people will be hard to achieve. The initiative's future will therefore depend to a large extent on its success in attracting investment into infrastructure projects.

From a political perspective, the PA's mantra of competitive liberalization stands at odds with other collective Latin American initiatives.

Although its members envision an inclusive and open approach to regional integration, their openness has limits: "We need to be careful not to associate ourselves with anyone who will hold us back" (quoted in *El Economista* 2014). As it evolves, the PA will likely consolidate an ideological orientation that further distinguishes it from Mercosur, Unasur, ALBA, and other contemporary endeavors. Key to the PA's orientation is a disposition to work more closely with the United States at a time when much of the region, not least Brazil under former president Dilma Rousseff, has sought greater autonomy and independence from traditional structures of regional hegemony.

Faith in the global leadership credentials of the United States is the common denominator underpinning the commitment of Chile, Mexico, and Peru to the PA and TPP. Political and business leaders in Latin America's three PA-TPP participants are optimistic that the United States will sustain a "rational and flexible" leadership role that will protect their interests. This, they believe, will enhance their ability to more effectively formulate and maneuver their foreign trade policies. The TPP is therefore viewed—domestically and collectively—as a litmus test on the leadership capacity of the United States.

Any bold predictions about the impact of the PA and TPP would be hasty and careless. From a Latin American perspective, it is more useful to focus on the agendas that have given rise to Chilean, Mexican, and Peruvian support for them. The specialist insights presented in this chapter open a window into these agendas, particularly their macroeconomic motivations. As the empirical evidence grows, it will be possible to assess how accurately our "epistemic community" of interviewees understood and predicted the outcomes. It will also become possible to consult with a broader set of actors, including think tanks, research institutes, and civil society groups, about the PA and TPP's social, environmental, and political implications. Strong differences of opinion are to be expected, but so is the gradual consolidation of a collective worldview that orients Latin America not only to the Atlantic but also to the Pacific.

3

Chinese Visions of Transpacific Integration

Jianmin Jin

UNDERPINNED BY THE PROLIFERATION OF FREE TRADE ZONES, REGIONAL economic integration is accelerating around the world. To avoid missing the boat, China is hurrying to solidify a global strategy that brings coherence to its economic partnership agreements (EPAs), free trade agreements (FTAs), regional trade initiatives, and domestic reforms. The Xi Jinping administration is sensitive to the national implications of regional accords and has resolved to promote Asian integration in a fashion that reinforces its domestic aspirations. This guiding principle conditions Chinese leaders' approach to all foreign initiatives, including the Trans-Pacific Partnership (TPP).

China's Ministry of Commerce stated in May 2013 that the Chinese government is analyzing the possibility of joining the TPP. The announcement should not have provoked as much international surprise as it did, since for some time China has been involved—officially and otherwise—in all facets of Asia Pacific integration. Moreover, the Xi administration has been steering China toward a more liberalized economic model that resonates with emerging structures of global governance. This is evident in the new investment agreements China is developing with the United States and the European Union and in the "negative list" and "pre-establishment national treatment" status afforded foreign investors in the Shanghai Free Trade Zone.

The chapter begins by considering the Chinese government's concerns about the TPP, an initiative that emerged precisely at a time when China's influence over East Asian integration was growing. The TPP has forced a choice on Beijing: join a US-led initiative or risk being excluded from a process that may shape the region's future economic trajectory. Next I argue that China has so far been able to respond to this choice with tactical restraint because, given the TPP's attempt to unify twelve countries with differing degrees of state intervention, financial liberalization, and international integration, there is no impending urgency for Beijing to act.

Chinese strategists are aware that their nation can influence the TPP's success or failure and that US negotiators would therefore like to see China eventually join. Four dimensions of China's approach to the TPP are identified and explored over the remainder of the chapter, ranging from strategic posturing vis-à-vis the United States to the prospect of using the TPP to energize the Xi administration's domestic reform agenda. I conclude that the latter aspiration is likely to bear fruit—to the benefit of China and the United States—if the two superpowers restrain strategic frictions.

China's Asian Integration Strategy

China began to actively explore FTAs in the early 2000s. Domestic opinion had been divided over joining the WTO in 2001, with detractors airing concerns of damage to the agriculture, automotive, and financial sectors due to market liberalization. The concerns proved unfounded, as these sectors remained untouched and the unemployment rate remained steady. With the critics largely silenced, the government enjoyed an amenable institutional and social environment for promoting free trade. The external environment, though, became less receptive to China's trade ambitions owing to a series of foreign antidumping measures against Chinese products, especially by Western countries, and increasing resistance to Chinese investment due to concerns of national security and technology outflow. The latter concerns have become prominent in the annual congressional reports of the US-China Economic and Security Review Commission.

Chinese authorities have come to realize that FTAs are important not only from an economic perspective, but also for their capacity to diminish fears of the "China threat" from the collective minds of other countries. This diplomatic goal reflects a domestic imperative: stable foreign relations permit Beijing to concentrate on China's economic development. China has therefore formulated its FTA strategy not for short-term economic profit, but to share and create profit with partner countries and thereby achieve political and social security. This effort to "buy security with money" is nothing new, as a similar principle also underlies the more successful FTAs advanced by the United States.

During the 2000s, US authorities began to show concern that their nation's presence in East Asia was diminishing precisely at the time that China was experiencing high-level growth and coming to the fore in the region. The Eastward "shift of gravity" during that decade is evident in a comparison of US and Chinese trade intensity with East Asia, which exhibits a significant US decline across the region's main economies (see Figure 3.1). The trend became clear just as the subprime mortgage crisis took hold of the US economy, shaking the nation's economic hegemony and strengthening Washington's case for accession to the TPP negotiations. By assuming de facto leadership of the TPP, the US government aimed to reinforce engagement with Asian markets while opening them to its exports and creating jobs at home.

US accession to the TPP interrupted China's strategy for regional integration by forcing a dilemma upon Beijing: jump on board a US-led Asian initiative or risk the disadvantages of being left out. Faced with this choice, Chinese advisers became concerned that the United States was trying to direct the evolution of Asia Pacific cooperation so as to share in the region's economic growth while restraining China's rise. Washington's efforts to cast itself—with the compliance of regional allies—as an instrument for "rebalancing" against Chinese influence was not appreciated in Beijing. The Chinese government nevertheless had to accept that relations with its neighbors had soured, provoking many to seek hedging strategies, the TPP among them (Yang 2013).

The implications and intentions of the US "pivot to Asia" have not been clearly defined by Washington, but as Kurt Campbell and Brian Andrews write, the policy heralds a "vast" intensification of US diplomatic, security, and economic ties across the region:

> The "strategic pivot" or rebalancing . . . is premised on the recognition that the lion's share of the political and economic history of the 21st century will be written in the Asia-Pacific region. To benefit from this shift in global geopolitical dynamism and sustainably grow its econ-

Figure 3.1 Variation of Trade Intensity Among Selected Countries, 2000 and 2010

2000

	Japan	China	USA	EU15
Japan	—	1.7	1.5	0.4
China	2.7	—	1.0	0.4
Hong Kong	0.9	9.3	1.2	0.4
Taiwan	1.8	0.5	3.8	2.4
Korea	1.9	2.9	1.1	0.4
Singapore	1.2	1.1	0.9	0.3
Malaysia	2.1	0.8	1.0	0.4
Thailand	2.4	1.1	1.1	0.4
USA	1.3	0.6	—	0.6
EU15	0.3	0.3	0.5	—

2010

	Japan	China	USA	EU15
Japan	—	1.9	1.1	0.3
China	1.5	—	1.3	0.5
Hong Kong	0.8	5.1	0.8	0.3
Taiwan	1.3	2.7	0.8	0.3
Korea	1.2	2.5	0.8	0.2
Singapore	0.9	1.0	0.5	0.3
Malaysia	2.0	1.2	0.7	0.3
Thailand	2.1	1.1	0.7	0.3
USA	0.9	0.7	—	0.5
EU15	0.2	0.3	0.5	—

Source: UN Comtrade 2016.

> omy, the United States is building extensive diplomatic, economic, development, people-to-people and security ties with the region. . . . Some have mistakenly described the rebalance as a "return" to Asia—nothing could be further from the truth because, in reality, the United States had never left. It is, however, a vast and dynamic increase in US focus and depth of engagement in the region. (2013: 2)

The trepidations of Chinese officials about this process have been deepened by US media coverage suggesting the TPP's capacity to build resistance against their nation's influence in Asia. Academic specialists have provided little comfort: Gary Hufbauer of the Peterson Institute for International Economics argues that "the U.S. wants to show the American flag will fly in Asia and we won't let China design the economic model of the future" (quoted in Davis 2011). President Barack Obama's public campaign statement that the TPP could exert pressure on China to follow international trade rules has provided further grounds for anxiety. Given the weight of US influence in setting these rules, Chinese analysts viewed this statement as a veiled attempt to impose Washington's will. Faced with antagonistic media, academic, and presidential assertions, Chinese leaders have adopted a subdued and cautious approach, biding their time to discern the true nature of the TPP's ambitions.

China as Silent Observer

China officially supports the creation of an Asia Pacific free trade region based on ASEAN+3 and ASEAN+6 of the Association of Southeast Asian Nations, and potentially even the TPP. This orientation was articulated at the 2011 US-China Strategic and Economic Dialogue, when the two nations agreed to cooperate and "share information" about their ongoing efforts to construct regional FTA frameworks. Beijing can express an accommodating view of the TPP with little risk because the agreement's implementation appears to still be a long way off. The compromises it seeks on tariff rates, service sector liberalization, and government procurement agreements (GPAs) will require protracted negotiations.

Only four TPP countries have so far entered into GPAs through the World Trade Organization (WTO), and efforts to encourage others to follow their lead face opposition from nations that are less developed and more reliant on government services. Furthermore, the economic inequality among the TPP parties will not sustain the apparent ambition of the more developed countries to fashion the agreement into an expanded version of the North American Free Trade Agreement (NAFTA). The collective gross domestic product (GDP) of North America, Japan, Australia, and New Zealand constitutes 96 percent of all TPP members, while the GDP of Singapore, Malaysia, Vietnam, and Brunei together amounts to just 8.7 percent of China's GDP, or a mere $795 billion (see Figure 3.2).

Given China's economic magnitude, the insistence of US officials that the TPP is not designed to exclude China is probably genuine, as a more beneficial outcome for the United States would be to open China's markets. It is therefore likely that US negotiations with countries other than China aim in part to pressure the Chinese government to avoid an impending sense of isolation and join the liberalization trend. Unless the TPP can eventually accommodate Chinese membership, its economic merits will remain distant from their potential. Meanwhile, China's attitude toward the TPP is subtly evolving, driven in part by Japan's sudden appearance at the negotiating table.

Perhaps to signal China's attentiveness to US priorities, on 30 May 2013 the Chinese Ministry of Commerce declared: "We will analyze the advantages, disadvantages and the possibility of joining the TPP, based on careful research and according to principles of equality and mutual benefit" (quoted in Boris 2013). International speculation about Beijing's apparent strategic shift generally missed the defensive nature of the maneuver, impelled by the changing regional environment and the need to secure China's national interests. Beijing's plan can be more accurately interpreted along four dimensions.

First, Chinese officials are aware that their US counterparts aspire to eventually bring them to the TPP table. Knowing that the weight of other emerging Asian countries is insufficient to achieve long-term results, China

Figure 3.2 Gross Domestic Product of TPP Countries, 2013

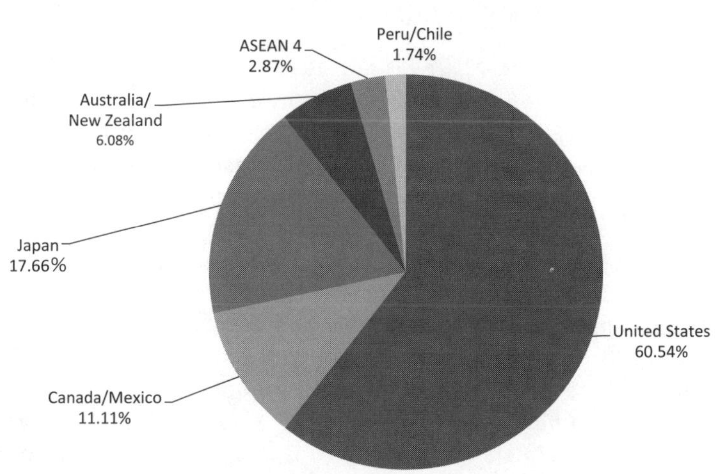

Source: International Monetary Fund (2013 dollar base).

is playing the role of silent observer. Its strategy may be to cede control of the TPP to the United States in order to generate a debt that it will collect later. Beijing is showing respectful consideration of US "profit security" with the expectation that Washington will be considerate of China's "core profits," and upon this calculus is seeking to build what Xi Jinping calls a "new type of great power relations."

Second, built into Beijing's strategy is an attempt to neutralize prospective US designs to contain China within the TPP's network of allies. As noted earlier, Western media, academic, and presidential statements that frame the TPP as a combined economic and security initiative deepen the perception that such designs exist. Many of the tensions that have recently emerged in East Asia result from a sense in Beijing that the US strategy is succeeding and demands an assertive response. But there is also a growing sense among Chinese leaders that a more effective strategy would be to cooperate with the United States, promote peaceful relations with its neighbors, and focus on economic growth as an enduring platform for regional influence. Simply put, cooperating with the United States over the long term will reduce the capacity of a US-led alliance to contain China.

Third, beyond its security and political implications, Chinese strategists are weighing up how the TPP might advance their nation's domestic economic reforms. Those who emphasize this perspective cite the benefits China enjoyed as a result of joining the WTO in 2001 (Ling 2013). The TPP, they say, could bring even greater benefits at a time when China needs to promote domestic consumption, climb value chains, and become more fully integrated into global financial markets. The main argument of this "structural shift" camp resonates with Prime Minister Li's repeated call for improved economic efficiency, premised on the belief that "reform is of greatest benefit to China."

Fourth, Chinese leaders are acutely aware that the TPP and the United States–European Union Transatlantic Trade and Investment Partnership (TTIP) are propelling international trade and investment into new territory. Since China is not directly involved in either partnership, its leaders are becoming more concerned that they will have no voice in the design of rules that do not involve the WTO. Because China has no influence over the TTIP, the shortest path for it to have a hand in the formation of global economic governance is to become involved in the TPP (Zhang 2013). From this perspective, TPP membership would ensure China's presence in the emerging structure of global trade policy, and in this way enable it to more effectively respond to US strategic ambitions.

The TPP text that was finalized on 5 October 2015 and publicly released two months later, on 6 December, is more a picture of compromise than the "gold standard" agreement initially envisioned by US negotiators.

The deal is consequently more palatable for members such as Chile and Malaysia, which have secured financial safeguards, and nonmembers such as China, whose long-standing economic reform process has turned out to align with the TPP in several ways. Thus, while the watered-down text could be viewed as evidence of weak US economic leadership, it can also be understood as a more democratic proposition that favors regional integration. Uncertainties remain about how members might move toward ratification and implementation, but the text affords insights into the TPP's relevance for China, particularly if it considers joining:

- The tariff reductions proposed by the TPP are unlikely to adversely impact China, whose 10 percent most-favored-nation tariff remains competitive.
- The TPP text emphasizes openness to foreign investment through the principles of preestablishment national treatment and negative lists. These principles will take time for TPP members to implement, and many will have long, negative lists for the foreseeable future. China, by contrast, has already set about adopting these principles based on the model of the Shanghai Free Trade Zone.
- China's government procurement practices would be affected were it to join the TPP. Although China has been working toward national treatment provisions for foreign investors (especially from the United States and Europe), the TPP would put its procuring state entities on a more level playing field with a wider range of competing foreign investors.
- The text on state-owned enterprises (SOEs) allows all TPP members to possess SOEs and requires that buying and selling is to be done on a commercial basis, with the notable provision that public services are excepted. This rule, which aims to ensure fairness between SOEs and private companies, is not included in general WTO regulations, but similar passages are present in China's WTO accession conditions. As discussed later, China has therefore been responding to this rule for some time through an SOE reform program. Among the resulting initiatives is to divide SOEs into public utilities and commercial-based enterprises.
- TPP members agreed that environmental and labor standards should respect international treaties and should not be loosened to facilitate trade and investment. As China has positioned itself as a prominent player in international climate negotiations, it has already factored the impact of multilateral agreements into its development strategy.
- The TPP text upholds labor regulations, as laid out in NAFTA, that protect the free formation of labor unions. This rule could cause problems for China under its current political system.

The TPP harbors no immediate provocations or obstacles to China's development, but its implementation would raise some long-term challenges. The Chinese government's reform program has previously demonstrated an official disposition to reorient the economy in favor of deeper regional integration. It is therefore likely that Beijing will maintain a cool-headed approach to the TPP while continuing to adapt national policies and take measures to mitigate any potentially negative consequences.

China's External Trade and the TPP

Chinese strategists have not twiddled their thumbs as the TPP evolves. To mitigate its potentially negative effects, they have proposed a scaled-up version of the ASEAN-China free trade agreement and pursued bilateral FTAs with Korea and other countries. China's FTAs are relatively flexible; even the most productive agreement with ASEAN (the ASEAN-China Free Trade Area [ACFTA]) has a large number of exemptions: 161 for China and 1,197 for ASEAN countries. ACFTA is producing results, but it is not a "high-quality" FTA because sensitive items remain subject to a 50 percent tariff. To deepen its regional presence, China concluded FTA negotiations with South Korea and Australia for enactment in December 2015. China's East Asian FTA network is thus nearly complete, with the exception of Japan. Furthermore, in November 2015, shortly after the TPP text was finalized, China signed a deal with ASEAN to upgrade their free trade area.

As well as prompting China to consolidate its regional influence, the TPP also appears to have stimulated Chinese regulators to adopt a more liberal approach to trade and investment, evident in recent high-level China-US and China–European Union investment negotiations. "High level" in this context involves commitments to pre-establishment national treatment for foreign investors, a departure from the current post-establishment requirement. This move also goes a step beyond the pre-establishment most-favored-nation treatment that China grants through WTO commitments and its 150 bilateral investment agreements. Furthermore, China has begun to implement a negative list for foreign investors that will progressively open up to foreign direct investment (FDI) in any industry not on the list. The previous positive list restricted foreign investment to a relatively narrow slate of sectors and projects preapproved by the Chinese state.

Chinese commentators and media exhibit a positive opinion of the shift toward investment liberalization. Wang Yong, director of the Center for International Political Economy at Peking University, recognizes that the commercial pressure brought by greater opening could stimulate greater industrial efficiency and competitiveness (Zhang, Chen, and Chen 2013). The Xi administration's policy to strengthen the economy through structural reform is generating the level of consensus necessary to drive international engagement. For instance, in September 2013 China announced that it would participate in the Trade in Services Agreement (TiSA), an initiative to liberalize services among twenty-three volunteer countries including Japan, the United States, and Europe.

China's commitment to TiSA indicates Beijing's proactive stance on liberalization. This stance is also evident in China's support for the sixteen-nation Regional Comprehensive Economic Partnership (RCEP), which as other chapters in this volume explain, seeks to integrate multiple ASEAN+1 agreements into a unified framework. Since ASEAN's GDP accounts for only 11.3 percent (2013) of the RCEP bloc, the participation of China and Japan are critical to its future prospects (Fukunaga and Isono 2013). As Figure 3.3 shows, China's GDP alone accounts for 43.2 percent.

Chinese strategists are wary that the complexities of integrating the ASEAN+1 agreements may slow RCEP's advancement. Given the uncertainties of the RCEP process, China has since early 2014 been advocating the Free Trade Area of the Asia Pacific (FTAAP), a framework based on the Asia Pacific Economic Cooperation (APEC) forum and originally recommended to APEC leaders by the APEC Business Advisory Council (ABAC), in which the United States has a strong voice. The FTAAP proposition therefore includes most TPP and RCEP members. By simultaneously supporting

Figure 3.3 Gross Domestic Product of RCEP Negotiating Countries, 2013

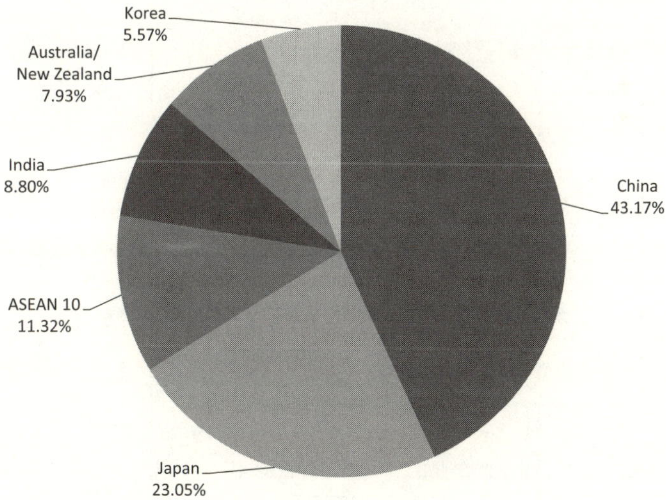

Source: International Monetary Fund (2013 dollar base).

RCEP, deepening its FTAs with ASEAN, and promoting the APEC-based FTAAP, China avoids the risks of placing its eggs in one basket.

Although RCEP and the TPP compete in some ways, their parallel development will accelerate Asia's economic integration. The simultaneous advancement of both frameworks ultimately supports the broader FTAAP agenda. While European and other non–Asia Pacific economies would be more disadvantaged by the FTAAP than by the TPP or RCEP on their own, APEC economies would conversely reap greater rewards. Peter Petri and Michael Plummer (2012) calculate that the removal of tariffs and the reduction of nontariff barriers between the United States and China would result in economic effects of 0.8 percent (TPP effect), 0.01 percent (RCEP), and 1.31 percent (FTAAP) for the United States, and –0.27 percent (TPP), 1.35 percent (RCEP), and 3.93 percent (FTAAP) for China. As long as the United States and China do not intentionally exclude each other, both will benefit from the FTAAP and are therefore likely to support it (see Figure 3.4).

Alongside these structures of multilateral integration, China has been pursuing an alternative plan for strengthening its ties with the Asia Pacific region called the "One Belt One Road" strategy. "One Belt" refers to the Silk Road Economic Corridor, which encompasses Central Asia, Russia,

Figure 3.4 Overlapping Structures of Asia Pacific Integration

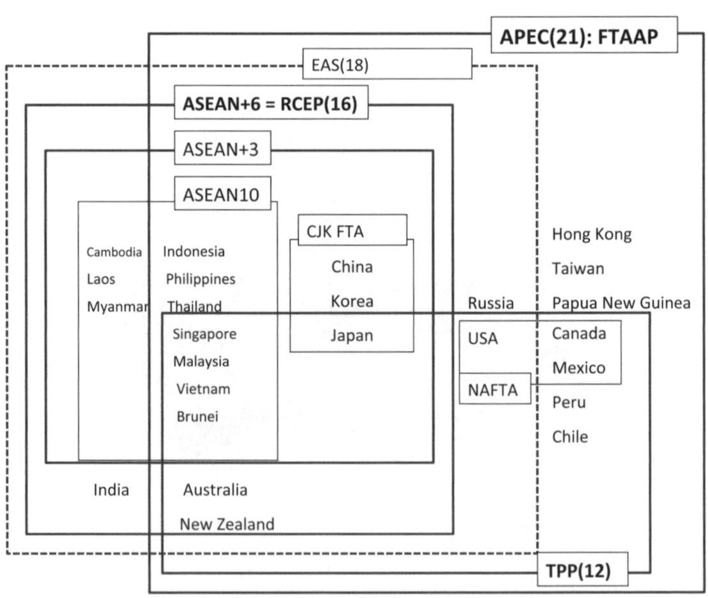

and Europe, thus connecting China to Western markets and hedging risks related to energy supply. "One Road" envisions a twenty-first-century naval Silk Road that spans Southeast Asia, South Asia, Africa, and Europe, securing China's most important sea lanes. These initiatives aim to provide a coherent narrative for explaining China's substantial (and growing) investments in foreign infrastructure, underpinned by new Chinese-led financial institutions such as the Asian Infrastructure Investment Bank and the Silk Road Fund. By contrast to top-down trade agreements, whose rules-based approach is epitomized by the TPP, these Chinese initiatives are literally laying the foundations of regional integration and connectivity from the ground up.

The TPP and Chinese Reform

Chinese authorities have begun to reform domestic systems in preparation for future liberalization. For instance, the Shanghai Free Trade Zone, established on 29 September 2013, relaxed market access in eighteen sectors (including finance, shipping, health services, and Internet services) and for the first time applied negative lists and pre-establishment national treatment for foreign investors. Despite the subsequent application of 190 administrative rules to the list—and the complaints this provoked from investors—the shift to a globally accepted negative-list method is significant. The government plans to replicate the Shanghai Free Trade Zone experiment, should it prove successful, to the rest of the country. This would reduce government interference in the economy and allow the development of market competition alongside independent legal frameworks for environmental conservation, credit, and risk management.

The negative list published at the end of June 2014 reduced the number of administrative rules from 190 to 139. Of the 1,545 foreign affiliated companies receiving new investment within the free trade zone (FTZ) at the time, 1,136 were established based on the negative-list system. According to interviews I conducted, the majority of China's local governments (more than thirty) are currently competing with each other to establish FTZs with negative-list systems. Their efforts in this regard reveal growing momentum behind the drive for structural reform.

Following the establishment of the Shanghai Free Trade Zone, the State Council published a document titled "Opinions on Promotion of Health Service Sector Development." The significance of the document lies in its application of a negative list to health services, stating that foreign investors "will participate in markets if not prohibited" (State Council of China 2014). The progression of financial liberalization in the health services sector indicates a steady march toward broader industrial reform. This trend in China's domestic economic governance has been spurred by the TPP and the related resolve of the Chinese government to prepare the regulatory foundations for an investment agreement with the United States.

Thirty years of economic growth following China's Open Door Policy gave rise to powerful interest groups that have become a force of domestic resistance against economic reform. The limits of reform are evident in capital regulations fixated on the state-owned economy, the Communist Party's control over SOE management, and interference in SOEs by stakeholders like the State-Owned Assets Supervision and Administration Commission (SASAC) of the State Council (see Figure 3.5).

There are many interpretations of "state-owned economy," even in China. Some believe that the main practical function of the term, like the slogan "protecting local industry," is to protect vested interests. For example, when the trade authority eased foreign investment regulations in the automotive sector in 2013, industry pressure groups widely publicized the need to protect national interests, effectively putting the initiative on ice. WTO membership has nevertheless fortified the desire of outward-looking officials to leverage FTAs and the internationalization they entail as a force for reforming SOEs and the financial structures they rely on.

Chinese reformers have espoused the concept of *dao bi ji zhi,* which envisions breaking through domestic resistance and inertia through the motivating force of the "external pressure effect." Their degree of success in this regard will become evident in the progress of China's investment agreements with the United States and European Union. It will also be

Figure 3.5 Governance of Chinese SOEs

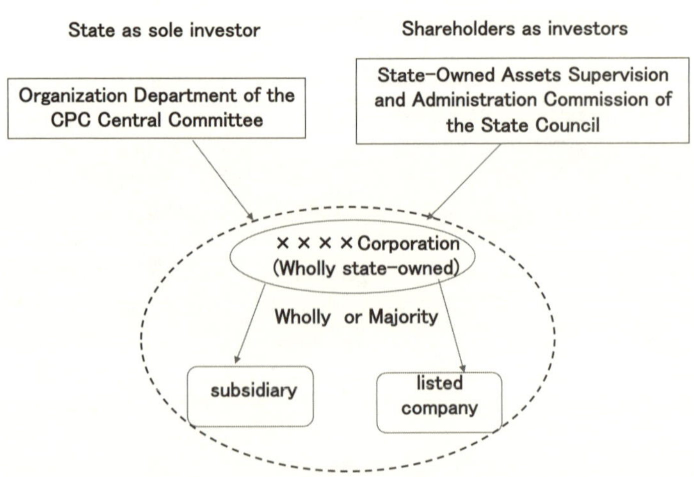

revealed in the gradual reconfiguration of the Chinese economy in a world increasingly governed by mega-regional initiatives like the TPP.

Conclusion

China's stance on the TPP is underpinned by a blend of international and domestic priorities. US motives for promoting the agreement are prominent in the calculus of Chinese strategists as they weigh up the capacity of its members to build an economic and security "containment net" around China. The public statements of US officials, scholars, and journalists that the TPP could advance this goal have deepened Chinese concerns. Despite its strategic risks, the TPP has attracted support among Chinese advocates of domestic economic reform. Just as WTO membership achieved a "jump effect" in trade and industrial expansion, the TPP could provide the necessary stimulus to improve China's "behind the border" approaches to regulating investment and stimulating free enterprise. This structural shift appears to be the most direct pathway to the "China Dream," and it is therefore likely to impel a gradual convergence of domestic development and foreign trade policy.

China has recently taken concrete steps to harmonize domestic regulations with international norms. Negative lists and pre-establishment national treatment for foreign investors are unprecedented in the People's Republic, and suggest a fundamental reorientation of economic policy to suit the pressures and opportunities of the twenty-first century. Likely next steps for the near- to medium-term future include more assertive action on environmental impact, SOE reform, and intellectual property protection. International observers are tracking China's progress on these fronts, and most recognize that although Beijing and Washington may espouse different approaches, their long-term priorities coincide.

The trajectory of China's development suggests a convergence with international norms of economic governance, and it has enabled progress toward a bilateral investment treaty with the United States. By identifying aspects of the TPP that might advance domestic reforms and serve national interests, Chinese leaders are signaling their disposition to work with the United States both toward a bilateral FTA and the long-imagined FTAAP. These goals are lofty but attainable if supported by the requisite political will, and for this reason all parties should avoid antagonizing one another's strategic sensitivities. Containment and coercion are known to score points in domestic politics, but sustained outcomes will require a genuine commitment to the mutual benefits of economic integration.

4

Contending Visions: The TPP, the Pacific Alliance, and RCEP

Barbara Kotschwar

WITH MULTILATERAL TRADE NEGOTIATIONS IN LOW GEAR THE BIG NEWS in the international trading system is the emergence of two mega-regional trade negotiations: the Trans-Pacific Partnership (TPP), which aims to unite twelve countries in the Asia Pacific region, and the Transatlantic Trade and Investment Partnership (TTIP), a trade agreement between the United States and the European Union.

The TPP represents 38 percent of world gross domestic product (GDP) (measured in current US dollars) and slightly more than a quarter of trade in both goods and services. The TPP negotiations, which concluded in October 2015, aspire to a "twenty-first-century" agreement that encompasses services, government procurement, regulatory coherence, and disciplines on state-owned enterprises. In his final State of the Union address, President Barack Obama called on Congress to ratify the agreement, stating: "We forged a Trans-Pacific Partnership to open markets, protect workers and the environment, and advance American leadership in Asia" (White House 2016).

The TPP negotiations have been officially portrayed—and are seen by many—as a pathway toward a broader Free Trade Area of the Asia Pacific (FTAAP). As such, the TPP could unite the Asia Pacific region in a true free trade agreement, a goal previously envisaged by the Asia Pacific Economic Cooperation (APEC) forum. The TPP is a big deal: in addition to its economic size, the precedents it sets in new negotiating areas could become the foundation for the revival of broader multilateral trade talks.

I begin this chapter by pondering the implications of the TPP for Latin America, focusing principally on the region's new major trade agreement: the Pacific Alliance (PA), a grouping of like-minded countries (Chile, Colombia, Mexico, and Peru) that as noted in Chapter 2 have begun to envision themselves as a collective "Pacific corridor."[1] I then compare the PA with a similar initiative developing in Asia, the Regional Comprehensive Economic Partnership (RCEP), of which China is a key proponent. Finally, I speculate on the possibilities for integration among the TPP, the PA, and RCEP and their potential to advance the FTAAP cause.

The Pacific Alliance: Latin America's TPP Nucleus

All Latin American countries participating in the TPP negotiations are also members of the Pacific Alliance. The PA has received considerable attention in anticipation of the formal launch of its trade agreement, its potential expansion to include Costa Rica, the addition of prominent economies (most notably the United States and China) as observers, and in general as a new direction for Latin American multilateralism. The PA has its roots in two trends: the increasing importance of Asia in Latin American trade, and the failure among the thirty-four countries in the Americas to conclude the Free Trade Area of the Americas (FTAA) negotiations, which stalled in 2003 and then sputtered to their demise in 2005. The first trend is illustrated by Figure 4.1, which shows that the share of ASEAN+3 (Association of Southeast Asian Nations) countries in total Pacific Alliance exports grew from $8 billion (4 percent) in 2000 to $63 billion (11 percent) in 2014. Similarly, as Figure 4.2 shows, the share of ASEAN+3 countries in total Pacific Alliance imports grew from $24 billion (10 percent) in 2000 to $177 billion (28 percent) in 2014.

As Latin America's trade and investment with Asian counterparts have grown, so have the number of free trade agreements between them (see Table 4.1). Alliance nations compose the vast bulk of these agreements, with several Central American countries engaged in free trade agreements (FTAs) with Taiwan. While the Pacific Alliance countries have some Asian FTA partners in common, the substance of their agreements varies. The PA could therefore play an important coordinating role.

The Pacific Alliance has evolved from the Latin America Pacific Arc Forum (LAPAF). The forum originated on the sidelines of the 2007 APEC meeting in Sydney as a cooperation initiative to enhance Latin American economic relations with Asia (Herreros 2011). It included the eleven Latin American countries with borders on the Pacific: Chile, Colombia, Costa Rica, Ecuador, El Salvador, Guatemala, Honduras, Mexico, Nicaragua, Panama, and Peru.

The Pacific Alliance came about in recognition of a split among the LAPAF countries. Those ready and willing to move more quickly toward the goal of enhancing trade with Asia formed the Pacific Alliance trade bloc, which was formally launched on 6 June 2012 at the fourth Pacific Alliance summit at the Paranal Observatory in Antofagasta, Chile. It was here that PA members Chile, Colombia, Peru, and Mexico signed an agree-

Figure 4.1 Pacific Alliance Exports to ASEAN+3 and Rest of World, 2000–2014

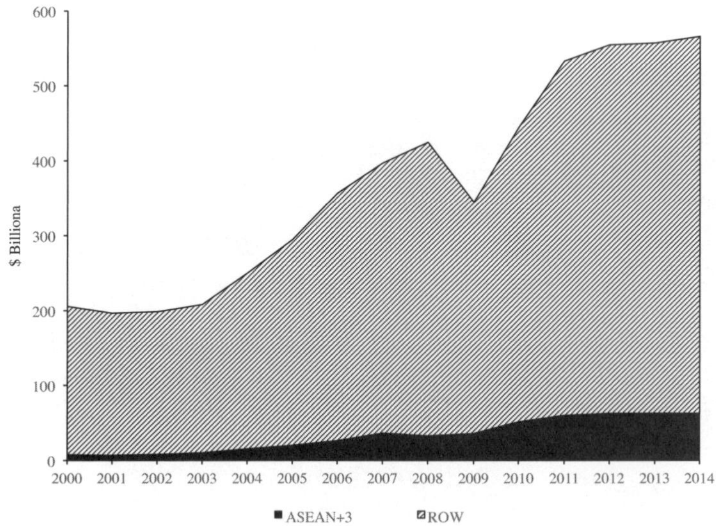

Source: IMF Direction of Trade Statistics.

Figure 4.2 Pacific Alliance Imports from ASEAN+3 and Rest of World, 2000–2014

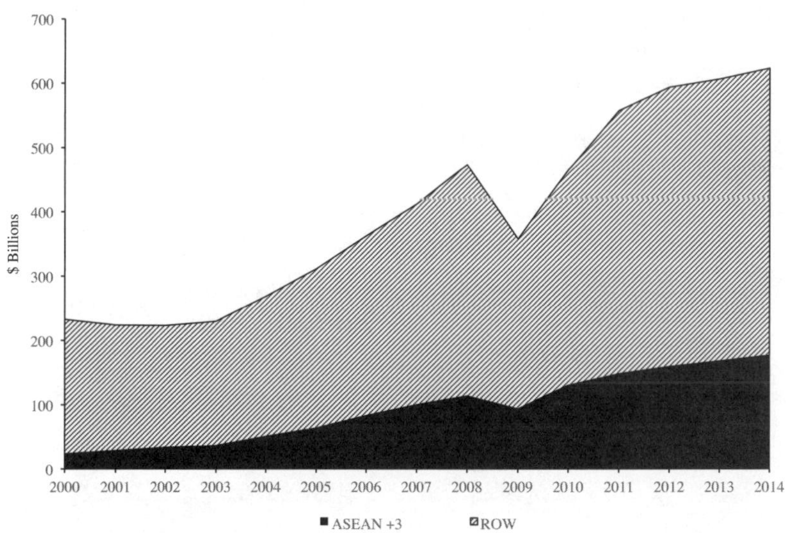

Source: IMF Direction of Trade Statistics.

Table 4.1 Latin America: FTAs in Force, Signed, and Under Negotiation with APEC Members

	FTA in Force	Signed but Not Yet in Force	Under Negotiation
Australia	Chile		Mexico (TPP), Peru
Brunei Darussalam	Chile		Mexico (TPP), Peru
Canada	Chile, Colombia, Costa Rica, Honduras, Mexico, Panama, Peru		
Chile	Argentina, Brazil, Colombia, Costa Rica, Ecuador, Mexico, Panama, Paraguay, Peru, Uruguay		
China	Chile, Costa Rica, Peru		
Chinese Taipei	El Salvador, Guatemala, Honduras, Panama		Dominican Republic
Hong Kong, China	Chile		
Indonesia			Chile
Japan	Chile, Mexico, Peru		Colombia
Malaysia	Chile		Mexico (TPP), Peru
Mexico	Chile, Colombia, Costa Rica, Panama, Peru		Mexico (TPP), Peru
New Zealand	Chile		
Papua New Guinea			
Peru	Argentina, Brazil, Chile, Colombia, Costa Rica, Mexico, Panama, Paraguay, Uruguay		Guatemala, Honduras, Venezuela
Philippines			
Republic of Korea	Chile, Peru	Colombia	Mexico
Russia			
Singapore	Chile, Costa Rica, Panama, Peru	Chile	Mexico
Thailand	Peru		
United States	Chile, Colombia, Costa Rica, Mexico, Panama, Peru		
Vietnam	Chile		Mexico (TPP), Peru

ment establishing a framework for a new trade and economic integration bloc, with a view to further linking their economies and establishing a platform for trade with Asia. The Pacific Alliance countries constitute the group that was most enthusiastic about the FTAA's prior ambition to unite the thirty-four countries of the Americas in a free trade area.

The founding agreement of the Pacific Alliance establishes the goal of economic integration among nations with democratic political systems, institutionalized separation of powers, and proven commitments to protecting human rights and fundamental liberties (Article 2). The agreement aims to (1) facilitate the free movement of goods, services, capital and persons; (2) promote growth, development, and competitiveness among member states with a view to improving well-being, overcoming socioeconomic inequality, and enhancing social inclusion; and (3) serve as a platform for political dialogue, economic and commercial harmonization, and integration into the global economy, particularly the Asia Pacific region.

The framework agreement of the Pacific Alliance entered into force on 20 July 2015. As of this date, 91.8 percent of goods circulate duty free among PA members; 3.8 percent more will be liberalized in ten years; and the remaining 4.4 percent in the subsequent five years. Learning from previous trade negotiations, the PA has adopted a flexible approach of doing what is possible, when possible. This is a refreshing change from the single-undertaking approach used in the FTAA and World Trade Organization (WTO) negotiations, which has ultimately impeded their conclusion. Liberalization of trade in services is under discussion among PA members, but has not yet been formalized. All of its members are among the twenty-three countries participating in the Trade in Services Agreement (TiSA) negotiations.[2]

Despite its cautious approach, the Pacific Alliance has been more ambitious than the FTAA in several respects, including in the liberalization of capital and migratory flows. Alliance countries have eliminated visa requirements for member citizens, authorized scholarships (provided by sending countries) to facilitate the circulation of students among the members' educational institutions, and opened their markets for up to a year for young people (age thirty and younger) to work.

The Pacific Alliance is open to other countries joining as long as they are able to fulfill its obligations, which include having already negotiated bilateral FTAs with each member. Costa Rica has come the closest: already party to trade agreements with all PA members, it began the process of joining in February 2014 at the eighth Pacific Alliance summit in Cartagena de Indias, Colombia. In 2015, though, Costa Rica announced that it would suspend its incorporation indefinitely due to a lack of domestic political consensus around the issue. Panama has also indicated interest in joining and, as of the July 2015 ratification of its FTA with Mexico, has FTAs in force with all members.

Alliance members are also moving toward greater financial harmonization through the Integrated Latin American Market (MILA), which for years acted as an interface for the stock markets of Chile (Santiago Stock Exchange), Colombia (Colombia Stock Exchange), and Peru (Lima Stock Exchange). It received a significant boost when Mexico joined in December 2014. By mid 2013, MILA comprised 26 percent of the domestic market capitalization of Latin American stock markets. Mexico's inclusion brings this up to 49 percent, on par with Brazil's stock market (BOVESPA). MILA includes about 80 percent of companies listed on Latin American stock exchanges.

The Pacific Alliance is linked to the TPP by the fact that three of the four PA members (Chile, Mexico, and Peru) are also TPP parties. However, Colombia is not involved in the TPP due to an unwritten TPP rule that limits the process to APEC members. APEC has maintained a moratorium on new membership for more than a decade: Malaysia was the last country to join, in 1998, but Colombia's request to join in 1995 was rejected. The Pacific Alliance therefore groups TPP members together with nonmembers, creating a hybrid composition that will deepen if Costa Rica and Panama (both non-TPP members) are admitted.

The Pacific Alliance's heterogeneity may complicate its ascendance, as those members blessed with APEC (and hence TPP) membership have gained improved access to external markets. Colombia has been mentioned as a clear candidate for TPP accession if the agreement goes into force, and may seek to implement disciplines based on TPP criteria to augment its chances of eventual TPP membership. To consolidate the PA's identity and purpose, the three nations that are members of both institutions will likely push to have Colombia invited into the TPP as its first non-APEC member.

Ultimately the TPP will bring benefits to the Pacific Alliance. Peter Petri, Michael Plummer, and Fan Zhai (2012) estimate that if the TPP is fully implemented, by 2025 Pacific Alliance members will have seen income gains of $1.8 billion for Chile, $16.4 billion for Mexico, and $3.3 billion for Peru. One would anticipate similar gains to Colombia and Costa Rica should they join the agreement.

RCEP: A Regional Response to Global Change

The Pacific Alliance is not the only regional integration initiative with a split identity. The Association of Southeast Asian Nations also groups together APEC members with nonmembers Cambodia, Laos, and Myanmar. To address resulting strategic dilemmas and advance integration within Asia, ASEAN has thrown its weight behind the Regional Comprehensive

Economic Partnership. First articulated in detail at the November 2011 summit of ASEAN leaders in Bali, RCEP comprises the ten ASEAN member states and the bloc's major free trade agreement partners (Australia, China, India, Japan, Korea, and New Zealand). Its main objective is an East Asia–wide trade agreement that merges two separate tracks: the East Asian Free Trade Agreement (EAFTA), which comprises the ten ASEAN nations plus China, Japan, and South Korea; and the Comprehensive Economic Partnership for East Asia (CEPEA), which includes Australia, India, and New Zealand. Negotiations among the sixteen RCEP parties began in earnest in early 2013. They were scheduled to conclude by the end of 2015, but leaders announced at the twenty-seventh ASEAN summit in December 2015 that talks would continue into 2016.

RCEP is a significant undertaking: its members represent 49 percent of the world's population and 30 percent of world GDP; they account for 29 percent of world trade and 26 percent of world foreign direct investment (FDI) inflows. Like the Pacific Alliance, RCEP aims for deeper integration among members, but its scope is not as ambitious as the TPP's "twenty-first-century" agenda, which encompasses governance of intellectual property, the economic role of state-owned enterprises, and other "behind the border" matters. RCEP's goal is to achieve a modern and comprehensive trade agreement that covers trade in goods, services, investment, economic and technical cooperation, and dispute settlement. An additional objective is to maintain and promote the existing sophisticated global production networks that exist in the region and enhance their competitiveness by reducing the overlap among Asian FTAs. These advances will allow ASEAN members free trade within the ASEAN market, as well as with the bloc's major trading partners.

While ASEAN has been RCEP's main protagonist, its largest market is China (Wang Yuzhu 2013). RCEP reflects China's recent strategy toward greater engagement in international trade agreements: China acceded to the ASEAN-China Free Trade Area (ACFTA) in 2010 and has recently established FTAs with trade partners in Latin America, Europe, and Asia.[3] These agreements focus on market access in goods and expanding access to services and trade.

RCEP can legitimately be seen as competing with the TPP by enabling China to consolidate its preferences in the Asian arena and to counter US aspirations in the region. It can also be viewed as an initiative that will help ASEAN countries—and China—prepare to meet the higher-level disciplines of the TPP. The two models reflect distinct approaches to integration: RCEP follows an ASEAN-style consensus model by focusing on tariff cuts and offering flexibility to members to proceed according to their comfort level, while the TPP contains strong provisions on trade in goods and services, investment, and "behind the border" issues such as intellectual property. Despite these differences, there is sufficient scope for the two initiatives to eventually merge into a broader Free Trade Area of the Asia Pacific.

Toward the FTAAP

The TPP and RCEP both seek to enhance integration among a large number of member states, whose trade constitutes a significant share of the world's total. RCEP's guiding principles state: "The objective of launching RCEP negotiations is to achieve a modern, comprehensive, high-quality and mutually beneficial economic partnership agreement among the ASEAN Member States and ASEAN's FTA Partners. RCEP will cover trade in goods, trade in services, investment, economic and technical cooperation, intellectual property, competition, dispute settlement and other issues." Like the TPP, RCEP aims for substantial coverage, from market access to investment, services, and regulatory policies. While the two are moving at different paces and with different intensity, their existence will have important implications for the evolution of Pacific trade. The obvious difference between the TPP and RCEP is the role of the two driving countries: the United States and China. Both are quickly increasing their formal economic ties with the members of each negotiating bloc, but only slowly with each other. China is not ready to undertake many of the disciplines set out in the TPP, which require a high degree of transparency and would involve upgrading regulatory policies. Disciplines on state-owned enterprises, labor, and the environment, for instance, are obstacles for China's eventual adoption of TPP-like disciplines.

The simultaneous advance of the TPP and RCEP has the potential to generate economic friction, political tensions, rivalries, and potentially incompatible trade disciplines. However, there is scope for cooperation if the two tracks proceed with a view to eventual integration. At their November 2011 meeting, leaders of the TPP countries set the goal of creating the foundation of a Free Trade Area of the Asia Pacific (see Schott, Kotschwar and Muir 2013; Petri, Plummer, and Zhai 2012; and Schott 2009). The TPP could provide essential inputs into this long-term goal, though its impact would be strengthened if its membership were widened. At present, the TPP intersects the Pacific Alliance and RCEP, but excludes important members on both sides (see Figure 4.3).

The most likely pathway to an FTAAP is a hybrid approach that links elements of the TPP to the Pacific Alliance and RCEP. Tensions could arise between the TPP and RCEP over the participation of key trading partners China and India, particularly in the short run. In the long run, though, the

Figure 4.3 Membership in APEC, TPP, PA, and RCEP

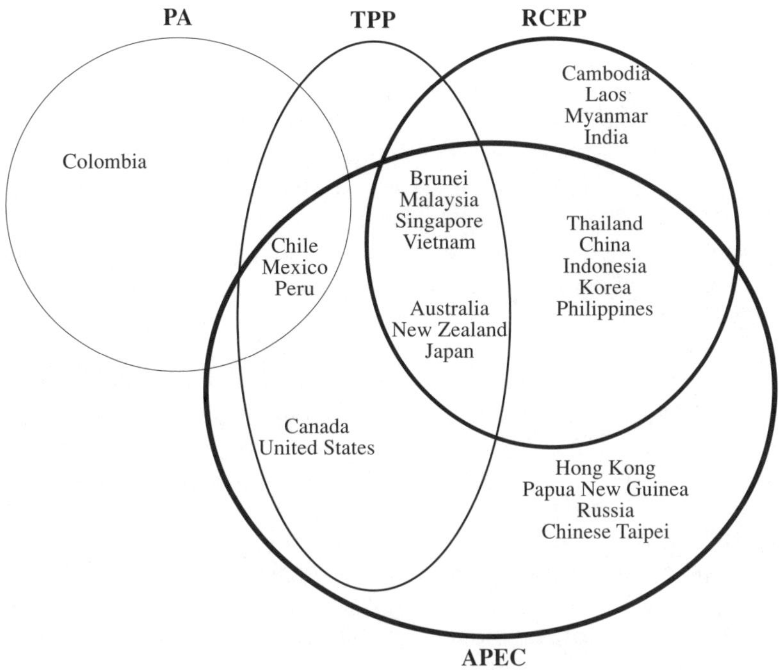

incentives would outweigh the costs and deeper integration would benefit the economies of all. Peter Petri, Michael Plummer, and Fan Zhai (2012) estimate that the TPP would bring the world gains of $295 billion (in 2007 dollars); RCEP could bring $500 billion; and an FTAAP that combines these agreements would yield over $2 trillion by 2025.[4] To achieve this hybrid outcome, US and Chinese leaders would have to allow each other some leeway with view to achieving not only stronger regional economic ties, but also closer bilateral integration.

Conclusion

In the wake of the failed FTAA negotiations, Latin America has become split in its approach to trade policy. While the Pacific-oriented countries have continued to negotiate trade agreements and open their trade and investment markets, the Southern Common Market (Mercosur) has taken a protectionist turn, and the Andean Community has basically disappeared. The TPP and Pacific Alliance reinforce this trend by formally grouping together and distinguishing those nations that seek greater economic openness. Recent political changes in countries like Argentina and an emerging discussion regarding changes in economic policy in Brazil may see greater convergence in the future. As Table 4.1 shows, Latin American countries have significant trade ties with one another; recent initiatives toward greater cooperation among the Pacific Alliance and Mercosur could provide a basis for slow but eventual convergence. Asia exhibits a similarly divided institutional landscape: four of ten ASEAN members are not participating in the TPP. This Asian divide could to an extent be mitigated by the RCEP negotiations, which seek to deepen ties between ASEAN's ten members and their FTA partners in the region. In this sense RCEP parallels the Pacific Alliance, three of whose four members are TPP participants, while Colombia and potential member Costa Rica are not.

While Latin America is working to deepen ties with FTA partners in the Western Hemisphere, it has not yet formulated a common approach to negotiating with Asia. The TPP and Pacific Alliance could lay the foundations for a more unified Asia strategy, but it is also conceivable that they could deepen the split among Latin American countries. Mercosur states and other like-minded countries have to date shown little inclination to craft more open approaches to trade and investment, and they have benefited from the policy space afforded through special currency and loan deals with China.

The most pragmatic path to global integration for Latin American countries is continued involvement in bilateral FTAs, the TPP agreement (should this become an available option), and engagement with the RCEP countries as they look toward a future FTAAP. A further pragmatic step is participation in new plurilateral agreements such as the Trade in Services Agreement, which includes Canada, Chile, Colombia, Costa Rica, Mexico, Panama, Paraguay, Peru, and the United States; and the 2014 Agreement on Environmental Goods, which includes Costa Rica, Canada, and the United States.

The best outcome for all would be a revival of the multilateral system, a prospect that depends largely on China, the United States, and other large actors. Ideally, the intersection of China's "community of common destiny" and the US "pivot to Asia" would end up being a rejuvenated WTO. However, China's recent economic slowdown could easily cause policymakers to prioritize domestic economics over engaging in multilateral trade and investment talks. The US election cycle has the rest of the world guessing at how strong US leadership in international rule-setting will be. Moreover, the TPP itself is not a done deal. The agreement will enter into force sixty days after all original signatories notify that they have completed their domestic ratification procedures. If this does not happen within two years, then the TPP will enter into force after at least six of the original signatories, making up at least 85 percent of the combined GDP, have completed and notified ratification procedures. This will require the United States and Japan to galvanize political support for TPP ratification.

As multiple national debates about ratification proceed, it is likely that the TPP's disciplines will have some impact on members' domestic policies. TPP implementation may change their position in global value chains, and they may therefore begin taking measures to optimize their future prospects for economic growth and development. The best path for Latin American and Asian developing countries is to adopt measures that will help them enhance competitiveness in the world economy and remain open to cooperation with a wide range of investors from China, the United States, ASEAN, Mercosur, and the Pacific Alliance.

Notes

1. Latin America's other major subregional trade agreement, the Common Southern Market (Mercosur), groups together the economies of Argentina, Brazil, Uruguay, Paraguay, and most recently Venezuela, with Bolivia as an associate member in transition to full membership.

2. The twenty-three TiSA parties negotiating as of June 2014 make up about 70 percent of global trade in services. These are: Australia, Canada, Chile, Chinese Taipei, Colombia, Costa Rica, the European Union (representing its twenty-eight member states), Hong Kong, Iceland, Israel, Japan, Liechtenstein, Mexico, New Zealand, Norway, Pakistan, Panama, Paraguay, Peru, the Republic of Korea, Switzerland, Turkey, and the United States.

3. China's recent FTA partners include Australia, Chile, Costa Rica, Peru, Iceland, Switzerland, Hong Kong, Macau, New Zealand, Pakistan, and Singapore.

4. Petri and his colleagues used Release 8 of the GTAP dataset, which includes data up to 2007.

5

Will RCEP Counterbalance or Complement the TPP?

Zhang Xuegang

THE RAPID EVOLUTION OF THE TRANS-PACIFIC PARTNERSHIP (TPP) HAS caused some disquiet in China, whose government is actively promoting its own vision of East Asian economic integration. The TPP agenda is considered by many Chinese policymakers and scholars as a centrifugal force initiated by the United States to rip asunder this vision, which depends heavily on the support of neighboring economies. From this perspective, the TPP constitutes a key part of the renewed US focus on Asia that may reduce Asian nations' economic dependence on China. Perceiving a US encroachment into its backyard, China has been actively pushing its own comprehensive free trade agenda in order to counterbalance the TPP (Yuan 2012).

It has been widely argued that China is responding to the TPP by redoubling its support for the Regional Comprehensive Economic Partnership (RCEP), which was first proposed in 2011 and officially endorsed at the November 2012 East Asia Summit (Hiebert and Hanlon 2012). RCEP aspires to be the largest multilateral free trade agreement (FTA) in the world, comprising all ten Association of Southeast Asian Nations (ASEAN) countries and the six other countries with which ASEAN has FTAs—China, Japan, South Korea, India, Australia, and New Zealand. Because RCEP was announced precisely as the United States was affirming its commitment to the TPP, many have concluded that the former must constitute a response—pushed by China—to the latter.

Considering the high financial, economic, and political stakes of the two negotiations, it is important to discern the extent to which China would be interested in—and capable of—using RCEP to counterbalance the TPP. This chapter aims to clarify this matter by evaluating RCEP's goals and prospects and China's role in advancing these. It also considers points of friction and convergence between RCEP and the TPP and the long-term implications of these points for the formation of the proposed Free Trade Area of the Asia Pacific (FTAAP).

Both the TPP and RCEP intend to capitalize on enhanced activity in the Asia Pacific region, albeit through different approaches to liberalization and trade facilitation (Celikkol 2013). The proliferation of frameworks for integrating the region begs the question: Which—if any—of these encompasses the greatest number of trade agreements and gravity of influence? Political leaders wish to avoid outright competition for primacy between the TPP and RCEP, as resulting tensions could disrupt Sino-US economic interdependence. Instead, they have articulated the more conciliatory and unified goal of advancing the encompassing FTAAP agreement. The inclusiveness of this prospect is appealing, but even the idea of the FTAAP is engendering Sino-US competition. Premiere Li Keqiang and other Chinese officials have proposed hard dates to commence FTAAP negotiations, but US and Japanese counterparts insist on concluding the TPP first. The debate harbors a simmering dispute over whose framework will encompass whose to organize the region's increasingly crowded "noodle bowl" of trade agreements.

I begin the chapter by assessing the main challenges posed by the TPP for its members, such as strict rules on intellectual property and state-owned enterprises (SOEs). I next focus on RCEP, and particularly China's role within it, noting Beijing's insistence that ASEAN is the initiative's protagonist—a stance that seeks to limit anxiety among RCEP members, and the potential for their defection to the TPP. I then propose that, in contrast to the TPP, the main challenge facing RCEP is its flexibility on trade and investment conditions, which may slow the consolidation of common purpose among its diverse members. I find that uncertainties about the future of regional economic governance have led the Chinese government to pursue a pluralist strategy that simultaneously accommodates RCEP, the TPP, and a range of alternative FTAs. Finally, I argue that the prospects for integrating the TPP and RCEP will be conditioned by the dynamics of Sino-US competition under the proposed FTAAP agreement.

Does the TPP Set the Bar Too High?

US officials have described the TPP as a "twenty-first-century" trade agreement, presumably because it includes a series of standards and conditions that differentiate it from other multilateral FTAs (USTR 2011). These standards apparently aim to transcend and circumvent the detailed debates that have bogged down the Doha round of the World Trade Organization (WTO). Deep-cutting provisions on agriculture, intellectual property, financial controls, and regulation of state-owned enterprises are some examples of this new approach. Economically developed TPP members with globally competitive enterprises will benefit from the internationalization of these standards, particularly in advanced segments of the agriculture, information technology, pharmaceuticals, and sophisticated manufacturing value chains. However, less developed members have expressed concerns that some of the TPP's rules limit their prospects for future development. It is in this context that the prominent online network Alternet has described the TPP as a "wish list of the 1 percent" (Sutherlin 2012).

As noted in Chapters 8 and 9, agriculture remains central to the debate among TPP member nations, with the Japanese government among the most vocal. Forty percent of Japan's domestic demand for food is serviced by its national agriculture sector, but should the TPP be ratified this share would likely decline to 20 percent or less. The predicament of Hokkaido, Japan's largest prefecture, clearly illustrates the implications of this adjustment. Based on a current import tariff of at least 10 percent on twelve different major agricultural products, Hokkaido estimates direct agricultural production would decline by $4.8 billion, fishing by around $453 million, and the pulp industry by about $33 million. Hokkaido's governing bureaucracy and the agricultural cooperatives that underpin its authority have advocated continued protection because, they say, the number of the prefecture's farms would contract by more than 50 percent, from 43,300 to 23,000, under the TPP. Rice farms would be especially hard-hit and could expect the loss of some 14,000 jobs (Johnston 2013).

The TPP would unleash unprecedented competition between Japanese and US farmers, but tensions with the United States would also extend to other countries. The New Zealand government, for instance, will face bitter domestic criticism if it cannot proceed with plans to set tariffs on US beef, and the heat will rise if the United States pursues its claim that New Zealand milk producers are violating market principles through monopolistic activities.

Intellectual property (IP) is another point of contention that carries serious implications for developing countries. The TPP's proposed IP protections, which are more extensive than those found in most bilateral FTAs, could impede Internet usage and the development of the medical and pharmaceutical industries (Flynn et al. 2011). In 2013 over thirty Internet freedom organizations including the Electronic Frontier Foundation and OpenMedia called on TPP negotiators to provide a "fair deal" on intellectual property. Over 15,000 citizens have joined the campaign, driven in part by concerns about the prospect of limits on the electronic dissemination of educational texts and resources. The proposed IP provisions could also limit access to medicine. Several nongovernmental organizations (NGOs) have pointed out that the extension of patents on brand-name pharmaceuticals under the proposed rules will impede low-income earners from accessing more affordable generic versions. Vietnamese critics argue that the TPP will not accommodate existing nondiscriminatory drug reimbursement programs or integrate with member countries' diverse health systems. The TPP's poorest members risk losing the most from the proposed IP rules, prompting ten US congresspeople to put these concerns in writing to US trade representative Ron Kirk.[1]

The TPP's attempt to reduce the role of state-owned enterprises raises serious challenges for Vietnam and other nations whose governments subsidize or operate public services. The reforms that would be necessary to diminish the role of SOEs could cause major disruptions to health, education, housing, and other critical services. As of mid-2016 it is unlikely that Vietnam is capable of such extensive reforms. In July 2013, Vietnamese president Truong Tan Sang made his first official visit to the United States, where he met President Barack Obama. While the two presidents reaffirmed their commitment to concluding the TPP as soon as possible, the above issues—not to mention ongoing differences over human rights—will continue to complicate this prospect (Hiep 2013).

The TPP's rules-of-origin regulations are yet another sticking point for Vietnam, whose manufacturing relies heavily on commodities, machines, and other intermediate goods imported from China. Under the TPP, Vietnamese manufacturers that export products containing these components to markets in other TPP nations will not be eligible for preferential access. It has been suggested that Vietnam's textile trade with the United States would grow by 12 to 13 percent under the TPP, but the validity of these figures will depend on how tightly the rules of origin are defined. The indications are that only a small number of Vietnamese enterprises would benefit from the TPP, and that the benefits they gain would be limited. According to Vietnam's main footwear industry association, state-owned enterprises account for 55 percent of shoe production, and 80 to 90 percent of the materials for the shoes come from non-TPP states. *Financial Times* columnist David Pilling (2013) notes that Vietnam's clothing exporters will face the same problem: "At the moment, of course, much of the cotton for Vietnam's huge garment industry comes from China. How do you design a club that excludes China but admits the likes of Vietnam? After all, Vietnam is also a command economy with huge state-owned enterprises, opaque regulations and a keen disregard for intellectual property."

Though likely to be affected differently, signatories must accept all of the TPP's provisions, at least in principle, in order to participate in it. This poses a problem for potential latecomers like China and India, which would have to commit up front to deep-cutting reforms. Presented with this challenge, China is exploring alternative pathways to multilateral integration. Foremost among these is the Regional Comprehensive Economic Partnership.

Reluctant Leader: China and RCEP

RCEP was first proposed at the nineteenth summit of ASEAN leaders in November 2011, when the ten ASEAN member states and the six nations with which ASEAN has FTAs agreed to establish a single comprehensive Asia Pacific regional trade mechanism (Su 2012). ASEAN was at that time considering two distinct architectures of regional trade. The first, an East Asian Free Trade Agreement (EAFTA), would include ASEAN member countries as well as China, Japan, and South Korea. The second, a Comprehensive Economic Partnership for East Asia (CEPEA), would also include India, Australia, and New Zealand. As noted by Tim Summers in Chapter 6, China advocated the prior more restricted membership. However, Japan favored the latter, prompting ASEAN leaders to strike a balance through RCEP, which allows new members to join in the future (Hiebert and Hanlon 2012).

According to RCEP's guiding principles, the partnership has "an open accession clause to enable the participation of any ASEAN FTA partner that did not participate in the RCEP negotiations and any other external economic partners after the completion of the RCEP negotiations" (IADB 2012). The current RCEP countries represent approximately half of the world's population (3.5 billion people) and $20 trillion in gross domestic product (GDP). Although thirteen of its sixteen members are emerging economies, RCEP is demographically and economically the world's largest prospective free trade area (*Xinmin News* 2013).

The first round of RCEP negotiations, in Brunei in May 2013, set the goal of establishing a modern, comprehensive, high-quality, and mutually beneficial agreement. In principle, these goals resemble those of the TPP, as does RCEP's commitment to creating an open trade and investment environment in the region to support global economic growth. The second round of negotiations took place in September 2014 when RCEP members agreed to eliminate trade barriers by 2016. This ambitious timeframe resulted in part from concerns that the TPP may compromise ASEAN's future relevance, a concern predicated on the involvement of four ASEAN nations (Brunei, Singapore, Malaysia, and Vietnam) in the TPP.

RCEP's guiding principles state that participating countries "recognize ASEAN Centrality in the emerging regional economic architecture and the interests of ASEAN's FTA Partners in supporting and contributing to economic integration, equitable economic development and strengthening economic cooperation among the participating countries" (IADB 2012). As one of the participants, China must also officially support "ASEAN centrality" in the RCEP negotiation process, and it appears to be content to play a supporting role. By facilitating rather than leading, China avoids a stance that would deepen international perceptions that it is trying to counter US influence in East Asia. Moreover, as Jianmin Jin (2013) writes, in Beijing's calculations ASEAN's lead will prevent the United States from eventually joining RCEP.

China's decision to avoid presenting itself as a leader of the RCEP negotiations is not unilateral. ASEAN nations are themselves eager to advance RCEP as a collectively led endeavor, in part because this approach is more likely to sustain ASEAN's relevance into the future. Were RCEP to become subject to Chinese leadership, ASEAN members might look more closely at joining the TPP, which would in turn weaken ASEAN's position as the preeminent regional institution.

While some relatively advanced ASEAN economies, such as Singapore and Malaysia, have joined the TPP negotiations, other countries whose economic growth and per capita GDP are lagging behind, such as Indonesia, Cambodia, Laos, and Myanmar, are still in no position to follow their example. Leaders of these nations would be hard-pressed to convince their citizens that the TPP's elimination of special treatment on tariffs, provisions on intellectual property, rules of origin, and state-owned enterprises are in their interests. Nevertheless, ASEAN's proponents worry that this could change over time and that the TPP could eventually attract more ASEAN members to join it. Collective leadership of RCEP is viewed as an important region-building endeavor that could prevent this.

Although China has not been willing to officially lead the RCEP negotiations, the initiative clearly resonates with Beijing's broader strategy of promoting trade and investment with neighboring countries in order to counterbalance US influence in the region. Hence, behind the scenes, China will play an important—perhaps the most important—role in advancing the RCEP negotiations.

The RCEP Paradox

It is one thing to articulate a harmonized commitment to reducing tariffs, but to achieve this is incredibly complicated. RCEP aims to forge one "super-FTA" out of the agreements that its members are currently involved in: ASEAN, ASEAN-China, ASEAN-Japan, ASEAN–South Korea, ASEAN-India, and ASEAN–Australia–New Zealand. The different tariff levels maintained by each of these regimes will not easily be harmonized. In goods trade, for instance, ASEAN initially aimed to eliminate tariffs by 2016, while the ASEAN-China FTA has been doing so for 94.3 percent of goods since 2012; the ASEAN-Japan FTA aspires to eliminate tariffs for 64.5 percent of its goods by 2023, while the ASEAN-India FTA seeks to do so for 74.2 percent of goods by 2017. Against this untidy background, RCEP's commitment to achieving higher zero-tariff coverage than any of these FTAs by 2016 was overly ambitious, especially given the influence of protectionist lobbies in many of its countries.

Despite the apparent similarity of their overarching objectives, RCEP differs from the TPP in several respects, not least the flexibility it affords its developing-country members in relation to market access, intellectual property, and agriculture liberalization. According to the May 2013 RCEP joint statement: "Taking into consideration the different levels of development of the participating countries, the RCEP will include appropriate forms of flexibility including provision for special and differential treatment, plus additional flexibility to the least-developed ASEAN Member States, consistent with the existing ASEAN+1 FTAs, as applicable" (ASEAN 2013). According to Jayant Menon (2013), a prominent economist at the Asian Development Bank, this flexibility clause could help achieve consensus during the negotiation process by allowing individual countries to protect their disparate national economic interests, but it could also curtail efforts to deepen collective liberalization.

The challenge of unifying distinct regulations is evident in the fraught issue of rules of origin (ROOs), which determine a given product's country of origin and in turn its eligibility for preferential treatment. Menon identifies at least twenty-two different ROOs among ASEAN+1 FTAs, even after aggregating those that are similar, and finds moreover that only around 30 percent of tariff lines across the ASEAN+1 FTAs share common ROOs. The difficulty of consolidating these and other discrepancies could pressure RCEP to embark on a "race to the bottom," where the lowest common denominator of all the existing ASEAN+1 FTA rules will apply. Under these circumstances, it is doubtful that the joint statement's promise that "RCEP will have broader and deeper engagement with significant improvements over the existing ASEAN+1 FTAs" will come to fruition.

As well as the difficulties it faces in consolidating existing free trade agreements, RCEP must also overcome opposition from entrenched domestic interest groups. The Japanese and South Korean agriculture sectors have been particularly vocal throughout the RCEP negotiations (Yu 2012). Meanwhile, India's manufacturing sector strongly opposes RCEP's proposed tariff reductions, since these could invite an onslaught of cheap Chinese manufactured goods (Sinha and Nataraj 2013). China's state-owned enterprises are also capable of lobbying their ministries (Song and Yuan 2012). The China–Gulf Cooperation Council (GCC) FTA negotiations eventually stalled due to the resistance of China's powerful oil enterprises, which would have suffered huge losses if China had significantly reduced tariff barriers on energy products imported from GCC countries. Similarly, China's state-owned automobile companies regard the China–South Korea FTA as a potential threat and may demand special consideration.

A third obstacle in the path of RCEP is the diverse economic and developmental status of participating nations, which will affect their readiness to liberalize. South Korea, Japan, Singapore, Australia, and New Zealand are highly developed and specialized in high-tech products and intermediary goods, while China, Malaysia, and Vietnam mainly produce low-end manufactured goods. Countries with heavily state-run service sectors, like China and Vietnam, will be reluctant to expose these industries to foreign competition and may advocate policies to protect them. This pattern is born out in the ASEAN+1 arrangements, which have seen South Korea, Japan, Australia, and New Zealand, respectively, commit to opening 85, 164, 85, and 116 service sectors, while China opened only 33.

Special consideration will be particularly important for China and Vietnam given their large state-owned sectors, and India may request additional protection for its software sector. These exceptions, together with the different tariff and ROO regimes noted earlier, raise a fundamental paradox for RCEP: to simultaneously accommodate the particular circumstances of nations with different degrees of economic openness while advancing collective liberalization, integration, and transparency. This paradox is the main challenge facing RCEP, and it will be magnified if members are permitted (as is expected) to choose between the RCEP regulations or the existing ASEAN+1 FTA rules.

Regional politics will also slow RCEP's evolution. Beneath the negotiating table lies a deep-rooted strategic distrust between China, Japan, South Korea, and other ASEAN nations. Territorial disputes in the South China Sea between China, Vietnam, Malaysia, Brunei, and the Philippines add a layer of complexity to the RCEP negotiations, and the wrangle over the Senkaku/Diaoyu islands between China and Japan in the East China Sea overshadows any talk of closer trade. It is unlikely that these issues can be quarantined from RCEP's agenda; indeed, deeper regional economic integration may well first require a measure of strategic compromise.

RCEP is a young proposition that will mature over the coming years. Its progress will be conditioned by ASEAN's own development and by the level of enthusiasm the region sustains for economic integration. It will also be heavily conditioned by Chinese priorities, which as I argue in the next section, are not entirely in line with RCEP's vision.

Chinese Pluralism: RCEP, the TPP, and Alternative FTAs

The scenario just outlined has led the Chinese government to adopt a pluralist strategy: advocate RCEP while simultaneously negotiating other bilateral and multilateral FTAs with neighboring countries. Chinese scholars and policymakers agree that RCEP is no substitute for their nation's other

FTA interests, such as bilateral talks with South Korea and India, a prospective China–Japan–South Korea trilateral FTA, and the ASEAN+3 FTA process. In August 2013, Chinese premier Li Keqiang reached an agreement with ASEAN leaders that their bilateral FTA should be upgraded and that the Chinese side would "strive to expand bilateral trade to $1 trillion by 2020," up from $400 billion in 2012 (*Xinhua News* 2013). According to Li, China would also strive to increase bilateral investment by $150 billion over the next eight years.

China has been eager to develop a closer economic relationship with South Korea, its third largest trading partner. South Korea is also interested in maintaining a friendly relationship with China, which is probably the only country in the world able to exert a measure of influence over the North Korean government's decisions (Hess 2013). Chinese and South Korean leaders are thus mutually interested in achieving a bilateral FTA. Meeting in June 2013, Chinese president Xi Jinping and South Korean president Park Geun-hye publicly reaffirmed this objective. Trade between the two nations reached $274 billion in 2013, a figure their presidents indicated they would like to increase to more than $300 billion by 2016. A month after the presidential encounter, during the sixth round of bilateral FTA talks, the South Korean minister of trade, industry, and energy, Yoon Sang-jick, stated that the FTA talks were progressing quickly toward conclusion (Bi 2013).

The proposed China–Japan–South Korea trilateral FTA is also progressing. According to Liu Jun, director of the Globalization Research Center at the China Institute of Contemporary International Relations, the parties aspire to establish the trilateral FTA before the RCEP negotiations are finalized (Hu 2012). This progressive approach is also noted by Zhang Yunling of the Chinese Academy of Social Sciences, who observes that the three nations have encountered difficulties lowering trade barriers in their trilateral negotiations, particularly regarding the Chinese service sector and the Japanese and South Korean agriculture sectors. Any advancement on the trilateral FTA will therefore likely facilitate a more comprehensive RCEP outcome.

Neither the TPP nor RCEP prevents participants from joining other free trade initiatives; indeed, Brunei, Japan, Malaysia, Singapore, Vietnam, Australia, and New Zealand are party to both. Some scholars have voiced concerns that overlapping membership will undermine the effective operation and integrity of both initiatives; others believe the two partnerships might come into direct conflict because of rivalry between the United States and China, respectively the main proponents of the TPP and RCEP (Basu Das 2013a).

It is possible that the TPP and RCEP could come to compete with each other, but this is not a foregone conclusion, particularly since trade between the United States and China is so important to both. US negotiators and their Chinese counterparts have for some years been crafting a bilateral investment treaty, and to achieve this they will need to build goodwill with each other. It is therefore unlikely that US strategists will shape the TPP agenda to conflict with that of RCEP. Moreover, any attempt by US policymakers to manipulate the TPP agenda in order to "contain China" would conflict with the interests of those TPP members who participate in East Asian production networks, which depend on China's ongoing protagonism (Basu Das 2013b). Similarly, China's dependence on US trade and investment will deter any Chinese actions that might precipitate fundamental disagreements with Washington over the economic environment in East Asia.

Overlapping FTA memberships are not a new phenomenon in East Asia. Among the TPP nations, for example, the United States, Canada, and Mexico have belonged to the North American Free Trade Agreement (NAFTA) since 1994. The United States is also negotiating the Transatlantic Trade and Investment Partnership (TTIP) with the European Union. Multiple FTA affiliations among TPP and RCEP members could ultimately bring the two initiatives closer together (Celikkol 2013). For instance, for developing countries such as Malaysia and Vietnam, the TPP and RCEP harbor similar liberalization challenges. If the long-term goal of the Asia Pacific Economic Cooperation (APEC) forum—achieving a Free Trade Area of the Asia Pacific—is to gain traction, reforms undertaken by these nations will provide the fundamental common denominator.

The Chinese government has stated that RCEP is not a Chinese-led FTA initiative to counter the TPP. Xu Ningning, executive secretary-general of the Chinese secretariat of the China-ASEAN Business Council, points out that ASEAN, rather than China, is leading RCEP's formation and that "the goal of promoting and establishing the RCEP is certainly not to confront the TPP" (He 2012: 7). To support this argument, Xu notes that among the ASEAN member countries, four have already joined the TPP negotiations, and that the Philippines and Thailand are considering doing the same. Moreover, according to Xu, it is not necessary for China to use RCEP to fight against the TPP because ASEAN has always pursued a foreign policy of "striking a balance between big powers" (He 2012: 7).

Having benefited considerably from global trade over the past few decades, it is unlikely that China will exclude itself from emerging attempts to promote transpacific collaboration, including the TPP. In March 2013, Minister of Commerce Chen Deming stated that China favors new approaches to regional trade so long as they are transparent and inclusive. The same year his ministry announced that China "will analyze the advantages, disadvantages and the possibility of joining the TPP, based on careful research and according to principles of equality and mutual benefit," and that China "hopes to exchange information and materials with TPP members on the negotiations" (Boris 2013).

Although the Chinese government is interested in exploring new forms of regional integration, it is wary of the risks associated with both the TPP and RCEP. China's support will be critical to the viability of RCEP, and perhaps also that of the TPP, but Chinese negotiators know they must be careful not to upstage ASEAN's leading role in regional affairs. Owing to the large number of nations negotiating RCEP (the ten ASEAN members and the six "ASEAN plus" nations), Beijing has no illusions of control over the initiative. Meanwhile, as other chapters in this volume point out, the TPP is widely viewed in China as part of a US strategy of containment. In light of these concerns, it is natural that China should exercise caution when considering its support for either agreement. While China's (then) prime minister Wen Jiabao announced in 2013 that his nation would fully support the efforts of ASEAN and its partners to establish RCEP, Beijing's reaction to the signing of the TPP consisted of a cautious affirmation that China is "open to any mechanism" that follows WTO rules (BBC 2015; Su 2012).

While RCEP harbors important opportunities for China to integrate more effectively with Asia Pacific economies and strengthen political ties at a time of growing tension in the East and South China Seas, it also poses Chinese policymakers with three key challenges. First, it pushes them to further open China's domestic agriculture, finance, and energy sectors to external competition. The same applies to services, for which, as noted earlier, China has so far opened only 33 subsectors to ASEAN, while South Korea, Japan, Australia, and New Zealand have respectively opened (or promised to open) 85, 164, 85, and 116. RCEP is pressuring China to downscale its tariffs, but Beijing's ability to bring this about is diminishing as sectoral interest groups gain political influence.

Second, RCEP compels China to speed up its efforts to establish bilateral FTAs that would enable the formulation of detailed country-level strategies and harness comparative advantages. China currently has FTAs with ASEAN and New Zealand, and in November 2014 it signed one with Australia. However, it lacks bilateral FTAs with Japan, South Korea, and India. The proposed China–Japan–South Korea FTA has seen several productive rounds, but maritime territorial disputes have impeded progress. The China-Australia FTA signals a gradual move toward Chinese service sector liberalization (including educational, financial, and legal services), but it is unclear whether other bilateral FTAs will expand or even match these terms. Until China can develop a comprehensive network of bilateral FTAs, RCEP may be seen by Beijing as moving too far too fast.

Third, RCEP puts pressure on China's leaders to reformulate their country's relations with the United States. Many in China believe the US "pivot to Asia" harbors a desire to contain China's expansion and that Washington is pressuring its regional allies, such as Japan, South Korea, Singapore, and Vietnam, to more clearly demonstrate their loyalty, not least through the TPP. The Chinese leadership is convinced that closer integration with the United States supports China's economic stability, and it is therefore reluctant for RCEP to be perceived—or used—to confront US interests. President Xi's proposed "new type of great power relations" reflects this double-edged agenda, seeking to articulate China's interests in an assertive yet conciliatory manner. The ultimate expression of this vision would be an integrated RCEP/TPP framework under the banner of a Free Trade Area of the Asia Pacific. As Jeffrey Schott and Sean Miner write:

> [China and the United States] are working together to prepare the ground for an FTAAP among all or most of APEC's 21 member countries. . . . Whether the driving force for an FTAAP will be the expansion of TPP to more countries, or some agglomeration of various integration arrangements in force or in preparation in the Asia-Pacific region, or whether the FTAAP evolves in a separate negotiation, will depend importantly on how the United States and China agree to go forward. (2015: 13)

The challenges raised by RCEP are not insurmountable for China because (excepting the great power politics of US-China relations) they are economic at their core. By contrast, the TPP's challenges are both economic and political. TPP provisions on banking, state-owned enterprises, governmental procurement, and intellectual property are matters not only of finance, but also of core governance. Copyright and patent protection rules could make it harder to produce and use generic medicines and to freely use the Internet. Rules on sanitary standards, such as requiring TPP members to phase out restrictions on livestock growth hormones, could compromise food safety. These and other issues require more consideration on the part of the Chinese government.

As noted, the Chinese government must also contend with indications that the TPP has geopolitical ambitions that challenge its vision of East Asian regionalism. As several of the chapters in the book suggest, this interpretation is not unique to China. As David Pilling (2013) observes: "No one will say it out loud, but the unstated aim of the TPP is to create a 'high level' trade agreement that excludes the world's second-biggest economy . . . yet somehow managed to accommodate Vietnam (an authoritarian Communist state) and Brunei (an Islamic Sultanate)." A higher level of disclosure about the TPP's strategic goals would do much to alleviate international suspicions, and without such disclosure China will remain cautious.

As it weighs the opportunities and drawbacks of RCEP and the TPP, China will continue to pursue bilateral FTAs. Its efforts to do so with Latin

America indicate a commitment to promoting trade and investment throughout the Asia Pacific region. China's FTAs with Chile and Peru have so far proven mutually beneficial, and other Latin American countries may find that their interests are best served by following this example. Indeed, Latin American nations interested in joining the TPP (as Chile, Peru, and Mexico have) may find that an FTA with China enables them to avoid placing too many eggs in one basket.

Chinese Views on Integrating the TPP and RCEP

Recent statements by Chinese officials shed light on their perceptions of potential synergies between RCEP and the TPP. Understood in the context of the signals they are intended to send to particular audiences, these statements illuminate potential scenarios envisioned by Chinese leaders.

Zhang Shaogang of the Chinese Ministry of Commerce stated at the RCEP and TPP International Forum, a 2013 academic event cohosted by the China Society for World Trade Organization Studies and the University of International Business and Economics, that China was becoming "more open" to regional cooperation: "The RCEP and TPP are the foundation for integrating the free trade zone in the Asia-Pacific region. . . . [China will] accelerate the construction of the free trade zone with a more open and inclusive mind and promote the integration of the Asia-Pacific region in an active yet orderly manner" (UIBE 2013).

While academic forums permit a degree of introspection about the need for less rigid approaches, the Boao Forum provides Chinese officials a platform to demonstrate their capacity to lead regional affairs in concert with broader structures of governance. In April 2014, Premier Li Keqiang opened the Boao Forum with a statement in support of multilateralism:

> As long as the TPP is conducive to the development of global trade and the fostering of an equitable and open trading environment, China is happy to see its conclusion. We are committed to upholding the central role of the WTO multilateral trading system in global trade development. Both the RCEP and the TPP should become important supplements to the multilateral trading system, and these two mechanisms should go hand in hand and reinforce each other. . . . As a Chinese saying goes, "When everybody puts firewood in the fire, the flame rises high." (*Xinhua News* 2014b)

Cooperative words are to be expected at a forum designed to demonstrate China's disposition to engage its neighbors, but Li's comments are noteworthy for their explicit recognition that the TPP could overlap with Chinese interests. He went on to advocate a feasibility study of the FTAAP, a point China took up one month later at the 2014 meeting of APEC ministers in Qingdao, when it proposed establishing a roadmap for the FTAAP (Zhou 2014). APEC ministers eventually agreed to draft a roadmap, stating in the ministerial joint open statement that to translate the FTAAP from vision to reality would require a new committee on trade and investment to "advance the process in a comprehensive and systematic manner towards the eventual realization of an FTAAP" (APEC 2014). The ministers also agreed to "formulate a roadmap for APEC's contribution to the realization of an FTAAP . . . and instruct officials to take concrete actions to produce tangible, meaningful outcomes this year and beyond."

APEC's enthusiastic statement on the FTAAP was driven, behind the scenes, by Beijing's perception that RCEP and the TPP might conflict with each other. According to Sun Yuanjiang of the Chinese Ministry of Commerce, the process of regional economic integration in Asia has been moving fast, giving rise to FTAs with different rules and standards. Therefore, it is necessary to "research and discuss the commonalities of different regional FTAs, so that these FTAs could become the foundation of forming a possible future Free Trade Area of the Asian-Pacific" (Zhou 2014).

Official statements aside, it is unlikely that FTAAP negotiations will start in the near future, since disagreements abound among APEC member countries regarding next steps. According to senior officials involved in the Qingdao APEC ministerial meeting, China unsuccessfully tried to include a target year for the FTAAP's establishment in the Qingdao statement. A majority of the APEC countries, including Japan and the United States, opposed this idea on the grounds that other major initiatives, particularly the TPP, should be concluded first (*Japan Times* 2014). Simmering below the surface of APEC's apparent consensus on the FTAAP is a palpable tension between China and the United States over whose proposal should encompass the other's.

Conclusion

RCEP and the TPP are set to refashion the economic (and to an extent political) architecture of the Asia Pacific region. As discussed in Chapter 6, their emergence may contribute to the "spaghetti bowl" phenomenon, in which multiple trade regimes overlap in an increasingly complex regulatory mix. However, because both agreements focus on "behind the border" issues, they are unlikely to become entangled with existing initiatives.

Despite their shared focus on "twenty-first-century" approaches to governance and investment, RCEP and the TPP differ from each other in important ways. The fundamental difference is the level of flexibility and special consideration afforded by RCEP to accommodate its members' different visions of development, growth, and state intervention. RCEP is therefore likely to be more attractive to ASEAN nations, since many are not members of "the rich country club" and owe their social stability in part to government health, education, housing, and other programs.

Though RCEP is actively under negotiation, it faces challenges that will not be easily resolved, such as consolidating existing regional FTAs and overcoming opposition from entrenched domestic interest groups. These difficulties have led China to adopt a pluralist strategy that seeks conclusion not only of RCEP, but also of other bilateral and multilateral agreements such as the China–South Korea FTA and the China–Japan–South Korea trilateral FTA.

Finding no advantage in directly opposing the TPP, Chinese strategists are instead promoting RCEP from backstage as an alternative that would indirectly weaken the TPP's impact. As Tim Summers argues in Chapter 6, RCEP seeks to diversify the regional economic landscape because "for Chinese policymakers it would be preferable for the TPP to become just one more noodle in the bowl than a dominant regional institution of which China is not a member." Beijing must avoid presenting itself as RCEP's leader or else risk fueling international perceptions that it is trying to counter US influence in East Asia. This would provoke trepidations in ASEAN and potentially undermine RCEP.

While there is room for the TPP and RCEP to peacefully coexist, some competition between them is inevitable, especially if citizens and governments continue to characterize them with superficial notions of "twenty-first-century standards" and "the ASEAN Way." Since it aspires to transcend the pitfalls of the Doha round, the TPP must stick to its "high standards" and require its members to espouse a common platform of reduced agriculture tariffs, greater protection of intellectual property, stricter rules of origin, and downsized state-owned enterprises. By contrast, RCEP offers its members an alternative "soft and flexible" vision of integration that is less singularly focused on trade liberalization than the stable interdependence of state and markets.

Over time, RCEP and the TPP could converge around a shared commitment to economic growth. This prospect is supported by the presence of seven nations, as noted earlier, at both negotiating tables. How these countries grasp or neglect opportunities to find common ground and transcend differences will play a key role in the dynamics of RCEP-TPP relations. Japan has shown more enthusiasm for the TPP than RCEP, in part because of its current government's commitment to free trade, but also because of its interest in building closer relations with the United States to offset China's growing regional influence. Australia, New Zealand, Singapore, and Brunei could provide important bridges between RCEP and the TPP, since they rely increasingly on Asia for their economic prosperity while maintaining strong security and cultural ties to the United States. Should Thailand, the Philippines, Indonesia, and most of all China and India eventually join the TPP, the potential for integrating the two platforms will greatly increase. For now, if proponents of RCEP and the TPP wish to articulate a common goal, they can confidently stand united in their shared commitment to strengthening the Asia Pacific region's role in the global economy.

Spurred by concerns that the TPP and RCEP may be incompatible, China is pushing for movement on the FTAAP. However, disagreements among APEC members, most notably between China and the United States, are impeding the initiation of FTAAP negotiations. While the idea of the FTAAP has long been advocated by the United States, China's more recent enthusiasm for this APEC-based framework reflects the extension of its pluralist strategy: rather than directly opposing the TPP, Beijing wishes to incorporate it into a broader structure that it can more easily influence. Whether or not China is promoting RCEP as a response to the TPP therefore depends on the meaning of "response." If it means devising a direct counter-position then the answer is no, but if it means broadening the context around the TPP to better shape its impact then the answer is yes.

Note

1. The letter, dated 2 August 2011, can be accessed at http://infojustice.org/wp-content/uploads/2011/08/Ten-Representatives-on-TPP-08022011.pdf.

6

Chinese Multilateralism: Diluting the TPP

Tim Summers

SINCE THE 1990S THERE HAS BEEN A PROLIFERATION OF REGIONAL ECOnomic and security institutions in East Asia and across the Asia Pacific, driven by a wide variety of actors and motivations. These developments reflect the renegotiation of regional order and shifting power relations in the aftermath of the Cold War and during a period marked by the rise of China (Goh 2013). The negotiation and agreement of the Trans-Pacific Partnership (TPP) can be seen as part of this process.

For China, one characteristic of the period since the 1990s has been a "turn to multilateralism" (Wu 2007) in the form of deepening institutional relations within Asia and beyond. This has facilitated China's engagement with the existing international order, for instance through United Nations peacekeeping since 1992. It has also underpinned Beijing's emphasis on economic development during this period. This can be seen in China's accession to the World Trade Organization (WTO) in 2001, which in turn provided a stimulus for domestic reforms that both acted as a foundation for economic development and helped China's integration into the global economy. This chapter shows how the unfolding history of this "turn" sheds light on the Chinese government's approach to the TPP in an evolving regional context.

Multilateral institutions constitute only part of the political and economic landscape in East Asia. Regionalization—the organic economic links that have emerged since the 1960s among the newly industrialized economies of East Asia and spread to include China from the 1980s (Dent 2008)—is at least as important as the development of regional organizations. Furthermore, despite the proliferation of multilateral security agreements, bilateral alliances between a number of East Asian states and the United States remain fundamental to power distribution in the region (Bisley 2012; Cha 2009).

The dynamics of US involvement in the region are clearly central to the TPP. Chinese concerns that the TPP may cement US dominance in the region have led some Chinese commentators to advocate further expansion and diversification of the region's already complex array of institutions, and in this way dilute the TPP's impact. The Regional Comprehensive Economic Partnership (RCEP), as other chapters in this volume show, is one such structure. This approach displays continuity with China's engagement with regional institutions since the 1990s in order to protect its economic and developmental interests. Development of alternative free trade agreements is an important part of this approach.

Recent statements by Chinese officials, President Xi Jinping included, have nevertheless suggested that there are already too many "noodles in the bowl" and that proactive engagement with the TPP is also possible. Driven by a sober recognition of the challenges facing China's ongoing economic development, this more conciliatory approach identifies the TPP's potential to advance domestic reforms in the context of the leadership's post-November 2013 agenda of the "comprehensive deepening of reform." I argue in this chapter that diversification and engagement are key ongoing dimensions of China's "turn to multilateralism" and that understanding these two policy orientations furnishes insights into China's approach to the TPP.[1]

China and Multilateral Institutions in Asia: A Historical Sketch

The first milestone in the development of regional institutions in Asia was the formation of the Association of Southeast Asian Nations (ASEAN) in 1967, followed in 1980 by the Pacific Economic Cooperation Council (PECC), which led in 1989 to the establishment of the Asia Pacific Economic Cooperation (APEC) forum (Zhang 2009: 10).[2] China's active engagement with multilateral institutions in Asia dates from the 1990s, following the end of the Cold War and in parallel with the establishment or upgrading of bilateral relationships with most of its Asian neighbors. China's accession to APEC in 1991, along with Hong Kong and Taiwan (as Chinese Taipei), marked its entry for the first time into a significant regional institution. The ASEAN Regional Forum (ARF) was established in 1994, bringing together countries across the Asia Pacific, including China, for the purposes of political and security cooperation. The Chinese government was initially uncomfortable with the ARF's cooperative security goals, fearing they were "driven principally by American interests" (Yahuda 2007: 78), but later engaged pragmatically with the institution.

Both APEC and the ARF spanned the Pacific. In contrast, regionalism *within* East Asia began to gain momentum in 1990. As the fault lines of the Cold War began to fade, Malaysian prime minister Mahathir Mohamad advocated an East Asian economic group, and later an East Asian economic caucus. These ideas were opposed by Japan and the United States (Beeson 2007: 228), but the subsequent development of an East Asian grouping consisting of ASEAN countries plus China, Japan, and the Republic of Korea (the ASEAN+3) took a step forward as those countries formed the Asian side in the launch of the Asia-Europe Meeting (ASEM) in 1996.

The Asian financial crisis, which struck in the second half of 1997, played a key role in strengthening East Asian regional identity. ASEAN+3 emerged as an institutional mechanism to promote financial stability and economic development, symbolized by the announcement in 2000 of currency-swap arrangements through the Chiang Mai Initiative. China's response to the Asian financial crisis, in particular its decision not to engage in a competitive currency devaluation, enhanced its credibility as a regional partner (Beeson 2007: 204). Post–Cold War, ASEAN expanded to ten members, taking in Vietnam in 1995, Laos and Myanmar in 1997, and Cambodia in 1999. ASEAN+3 then brought together almost all of what is commonly understood as the geographical East Asian region. There has been some debate about the leadership dynamics within the grouping, with Rodolfo Severino (2012) suggesting that the leadership role of ASEAN is much underestimated. This debate is relevant to China's engagement with East Asia, particularly in light of concerns expressed by the United States and several other countries that China's influence over regional affairs may become too prominent. The contested question of "leadership" remains an important part of the negotiation of the regional order, of which institutions form one part.

The collapse of the Soviet Union not only reconfigured international relations in Southeast Asia, but also led to the formation of the new Central Asian republics (the "Stans") on China's western borders. China pursued a more proactive and formative approach to regional integration in Central Asia than in East Asia. This is evident in the 1996 formation of the Shanghai Five and in its institutionalization as the Shanghai Cooperation Organization (SCO) in 2001 with the addition of Uzbekistan. China was instrumental in the SCO's formation and has arguably been the prime mover ever since, albeit in the context of a formal emphasis on equality and consensus among members.

China's recent commitment to engaging with Central Asia is evident in its attempt to articulate and construct a Eurasian Silk Road economic belt alongside a twenty-first-century maritime Silk Road, together underpinning the Belt and Road Initiative (Summers 2016). South Asia does not yet feature prominently in China's regionalism, partly because of complex bilateral relationships but also because of the limited steps taken toward building regional institutions in South Asia itself.[3]

Chinese multilateralism has developed in the context of a foreign policy that places growing emphasis on relations with Asian neighbors. A "good neighbor" policy was set out at the fifteenth national Party Congress in 1997, and it was elevated to the second most important task in foreign affairs at the sixteenth congress in 2002 (Ye 2010: 4–5).[4] In 2000, then-premier Zhu Rongji spoke of ASEAN+3 as the main channel for regional cooperation in East Asia, a sentiment repeated by his successor, Wen Jiabao, in 2003. However, Zhu also proposed a free trade framework agreement between China and the countries of ASEAN, an ASEAN+1 structure that was subsequently pursued by other major regional players such as Japan and India. This demonstrates an enduring feature both of Asian regionalism and of Chinese policy, namely simultaneous engagement in overlapping institutions.

In 2004, the Chinese government "took the lead in proposing the establishment of an East Asian Community, to be based, presumably, on the ASEAN+3," but this suggestion met with resistance from elsewhere in the region and from the United States, and China ultimately "had to give way to pressure from Japan and Singapore to expand membership to include Australia, New Zealand, and India" (Yahuda 2007: 79). This ASEAN+6 grouping became the basis for the first East Asia Summit in 2005 in Malaysia. China participated proactively despite its preference for the more limited ASEAN+3 structure, though some Chinese scholars have made a virtue out of necessity and talked about the summit as a "shell" to protect the "core" institution, ASEAN+3 (Su Hao, cited in Beeson and Li 2012: 41). Both ASEAN+3 and ASEAN+6 have provided frameworks for discussions about establishing free trade areas, known respectively as the East Asia Free Trade Agreement and the Comprehensive Economic Partnership for East Asia (subsequently the Regional Comprehensive Economic Partnership).

A flexible Chinese approach was made easier by the large overlap in scope and objectives of these regional institutions. The primary goals for the various "ASEAN plus" arrangements have been economic and commercial, reducing barriers to trade and investment, promoting common development, and promoting cooperation between member economies, though the precise nature of the arrangements has varied. From a strategic perspective, China's engagement with all of these institutions has helped it enhance its regional position and reduce—though certainly not eliminate—concerns about the threats or challenges posed by China's economic development and its potential disruption to regional order. While economics has dominated, the examples of the SCO and Chinese involvement in the ARF show that China has been willing to engage in regional security cooperation. Of course, China's prime mover status in the SCO and the focus of this organization on domestic security, Islamist extremism, and ethnic separatism have created a very different dynamic from that in East Asia, where traditional security concerns or maritime disputes between states dominate the agenda.

Chinese officials have generally preferred to talk about "regional cooperation" (*diqu / quyu hezuo*) rather than "integration" (Beeson and Li 2012: 37).[5] As Chien-peng Chung (2008) has argued, the extent of China's support for regional institutionalization depends on the distribution of power among the participants of a given initiative, the relative weight of associated issues for China and the other participants, and the disposition of the major players to support Chinese interests. These factors, Chung argues, have influenced the degree of institutionalization achieved by such initiatives as the Six-Party Talks on the Korean peninsula, ASEAN+3, and the SCO. China wields respectively lower to higher degrees of influence in these forums, which reflect lower to higher degrees of institutionalization. Chung's argument is further born out by China's greater disposition to institutionalize cooperation through ASEAN+1 than ASEAN+6.[6]

Several themes relevant to the TPP emerge from this brief account of Chinese approaches to regional multilateralism. A core theme is the contested and overlapping geographical scope of Asian regional institutions, from ASEAN+1 to ASEAN+3, ASEAN+6, the East Asia summit, and broader transpacific entities such as APEC. Especially relevant to China is the question of relative authority for institutions geographically situated *within* East Asia and those that span the Asia Pacific. For Chinese policymakers, these ambiguities raise questions about the role of the United States in regional institutions and in East Asia more broadly.

The TPP and US Rebalancing

The Barack Obama administration's post-2009 "rebalancing" to Asia has added a layer of complexity to Asian regionalism. In addition to closer military cooperation with Australia and several East Asian nations, the United States has demonstrated a renewed interest in the region's evolving multilateral institutions. In 2009 it signed the ASEAN Treaty of Amity and Cooperation, a necessary precursor to participation in the East Asia Summit, which it joined in 2011 along with Russia. It also injected new life into the TPP by formally joining the negotiations and catalyzing a November 2011 agreement among the nine member countries (at the time) to outline a framework of key milestones necessary for conclusion. US national security adviser Tom Donilon (2013) subsequently stated that the TPP was central to the US "rebalancing" to Asia, a sentiment subsequently echoed by other US officials.

For the Chinese government this was a significant and worrying development. It marked the first time that China had not been at the table in a *major* regional institution involving East Asia since it joined APEC in 1991.[7] Aside from its possible impact on trade and investment, Chinese policymakers claimed the TPP harbored the potential to undermine the "ASEAN plus" system, particularly ASEAN+3, which had been central to Chinese engagement in regional economic cooperation (Qian 2013).

The TPP adds another layer to the lineup of East Asian institutions. To employ the oft-used metaphor, it is another "noodle in the bowl" that further complicates the array of overlapping regional economic arrangements. But the TPP is also more than another noodle, since it has changed the dynamics of existing institutions, including posing a potential challenge to ASEAN, only four of whose members belong to the TPP. It has also hastened the emergence of the ASEAN-based Regional Comprehensive Economic Partnership out of ASEAN+6. With strong support from China, this process was formalized in a November 2012 accord among the sixteen ASEAN+6 countries to harmonize their existing agreements, namely the ASEAN+1 structures that China first spearheaded. This complex undertaking aims to produce a different sort of agreement to the TPP, one that embodies ASEAN's principle of consensual decisionmaking and, partly as a result, avoids the sensitive "behind the border" issues that characterize the TPP. As such, RCEP and the TPP are not compatible, in the short term at least, even though they are both presented as stepping stones to a broader Asia Pacific FTA (Song 2013).

Chinese officials continue to affirm that they welcome US presence in the region (Yahuda 2007: 81; Wang Yi 2013). But the TPP has raised the stakes, and the US "rebalance" has intensified China's ambivalence toward US influence. Leaving aside for the moment questions as to whether the TPP would benefit from China's participation (Posen 2014; Huang 2014), the Chinese response has demonstrated continuity through the use of two foreign policy strategies, namely diversification and engagement.

Diversification and Engagement: Two Chinese Approaches

Chinese commentators were initially suspicious that the TPP's provisions on state-owned enterprises and intellectual property would exclude their country from emerging structures of regional trade and investment. They also expressed concern about the TPP's potential impact on other regional initiatives. As other chapters in this book show, these concerns gave rise to a wave of criticism in 2012 and 2013 that portrayed the TPP as a tool of US power projection in Asia and an attempt to "contain" China.

President Xi Jinping's October 2013 APEC speech took a more balanced tone. It outlined a vision of Asia Pacific integration premised on openness to free trade agreements, innovation, and multilateral coordination to diminish the "spaghetti bowl" phenomenon (Frost 2013; Xi 2013). This vision hints at China's discomfort with yet another East Asian trade agreement, particularly one that could divide rather than unite. However, by recognizing the need for openness and innovation, it also hints at a greater disposition to work with extra-regional partners and to think more creatively about the content of trade and investment negotiations.

China's interest in institutional diversification in the Asia Pacific is driven by concerns that the TPP could introduce unwanted complexity into an already complex environment. A core component of this strategy is RCEP, which would enable China to advance regionalism *within* East Asia, opening parallel and potentially alternative avenues of trade and investment to the TPP. While acknowledging that RCEP is formally an ASEAN-led process, Chinese policymakers including Premier Li Keqiang have been putting more effort into it, for instance by explicitly endorsing it at the November 2013 East Asia Summit in Brunei.

Another component of China's diversification strategy is renewed enthusiasm for APEC (Bowles 2014), evident in the Chinese government's October 2013 statement that APEC can play a key role in advancing "transparent and open regionalism" (Chinese Ministry of Foreign Affairs 2013). This emphasis on transparency appears to be a veiled criticism of the TPP, whose closed negotiations evoked bitter public criticism around the world. Moreover, Xi Jinping called for APEC to play a leading and coordinating role in Asia Pacific cooperation, including the coordination of regional free trade arrangements. As APEC chair in 2014, China aimed to promote the institution's importance for East Asia, contributing to an even more diverse set of regional commitments, among which the TPP is but one. As a result, China has been promoting the APEC-wide Free Trade Area of Asia Pacific (FTAAP) (Das 2016), described by one Chinese expert as being able to "provide an overarching framework that transcends the narrative of competition between the Trans-Pacific Partnership (TPP) and Regional Comprehensive Economic Partnership (RCEP)" (Chen 2015).

Several proposed East Asian free trade agreements, such as that under negotiation between China, Japan, and South Korea, are also set to draw emphasis from the TPP. The three governments signaled the importance they ascribe to the deal in November 2012, when after a decade of technical research (State Council of China 2012), their commerce ministers sat down to negotiate despite the unfolding Sino-Japanese standoff over the Senkaku/Diaoyu islands. Tensions between China and Japan, between China and the Republic of Korea, and between Korea and Japan could yet derail the trilateral deal, as could the possibility of Korea's accession to the TPP (*Chosun Media* 2013). However, any progress on a deal with Japan and South Korea would suit China's aim of strengthening regionalism within East Asia, preparing the ground for an ASEAN+3 free trade agreement, and constructing a diverse environment in which the TPP must contend with a range of parallel agreements.

One existing parallel agreement that China appears eager to strengthen is the China-ASEAN Free Trade Area (CAFTA). As the first regional ASEAN+1 structure, CAFTA was important both in stimulating East Asian integration and in giving China a leading position in this process. In September 2013, Premier Li Keqiang proposed that CAFTA be "upgraded," apparently with the goal of consolidating China's position at a time when its relations with several Southeast Asian countries, particularly the Philippines, have been complicated by the reemergence of maritime disputes.

Another existing institution that could possibly be revived by Chinese interest is the WTO, though this will be challenging. China made a surprise announcement in September 2013 that it would like to participate in the hitherto moribund plurilateral negotiations on the Trade in Services Agreement (TiSA). This signals that China is looking internally at services reform, a development that could pave the way toward a full multilateral services agreement under the WTO (Drake-Brockman 2013). Should they be reinvigorated by fresh Chinese commitments, CAFTA and the WTO would both augment China's already substantial influence over East Asian trade and investment, with the corollary that the TPP's regional impact would diminish.

Finally, the growing emphasis in Chinese foreign policy through 2015 on the Belt and Road (or One Belt One Road) Initiative, and the accompanying Asian Infrastructure Investment Bank, can be interpreted as driven at least partly by a desire to deepen integration among Asian countries, as well as those farther afield in Eurasia, the Middle East, and Africa, thus diluting the TPP's impact (He 2015). The Belt and Road Initiative's inclusive emphasis on infrastructure development may do more for regional development by removing barriers to supply chains more quickly and flexibly than formal agreements such as the TPP (Elek 2015).

Chinese attempts to further diversify the regional institutional architecture and dilute the TPP's impact are motivated largely by the latter's high standards of liberalization, which may impede China's accession in the near future. However, in the long term this could change. The Ministry of Commerce has signaled that it will study the pros and cons of joining the TPP (*Caixin Online* 2013), and Ministry of Foreign Affairs spokesperson Hong Lei has said that China is "open-minded" about the TPP (*China Daily* 2013), a message also conveyed at strategic dialogues with the United States. Engagement with the TPP appears to be on China's medium-term radar, and Chinese commentators have called for their government to state its interest in joining (*Global Times* 2013a; Li 2013). When the TPP agreement was announced in October 2015, the Ministry of Commerce described it in conciliatory terms as "one of the key free trade agreements for the Asia-Pacific region" (*Xinhua News* 2015).

Chinese commentary suggests that one of the objectives of the China (Shanghai) Pilot Free Trade Zone, formally launched in September 2013 and followed in 2015 by the establishment of similar zones in Guangdong, Fujian, and Tianjin, is to undertake trial approaches to economic liberalization that could help China either prepare for entry into the TPP negotiations or deal with the challenges posed by it (*Caixin Online* 2013; He 2015). The zones will adopt a negative-list approach and afford foreign investors national treatment. Both of these conditions have also been agreed in principle as part of the US-China negotiations on a bilateral investment treaty, launched at the US-China Strategic and Economic Dialogue in July 2013. These developments, as well as eventual TPP membership, could chime with China's ongoing reforms in a number of areas: financial sector reform, reducing the influence of state-owned enterprises in the economy, and greater opening to foreign businesses.

Conclusion

China's past interactions with Asian and Asia Pacific multilateral institutions provide insights into its stance toward the TPP. Accession to APEC in 1991 was the first in a series of steps toward China's regional engagement, marked by participation in the security-oriented ASEAN Regional Forum in 1994, endorsement of ASEAN+3 and articulation of the "good neighbor" policy in 1997, establishment of ASEAN+1 and contribution to the Chiang Mai Initiative in 2000, creation of the Shanghai Cooperation Organization in 2001, and pragmatic acceptance of the broader East Asia Summit (which included Australia, New Zealand, and India) in 2005. In hindsight, China's "turn to multilateralism" since the early 1990s has consolidated its position as an influential player in the formation and development of regional institutions.

Chinese policymakers are concerned that the TPP could have a negative impact on their nation's economic engagement with Asia. The TPP also brings to the fore ongoing contestation of the geography and membership of Asian regional institutions, in particular the tensions between Asia Pacific and East Asian structures. Part of the strategy for dealing with this is diversification, as the Chinese government puts greater emphasis into the further development of regional institutions that might either compete with the TPP or dilute its impact, as well as bilateral free trade agreements in Asia.

Despite the misgivings of Chinese officials toward the TPP, recent statements on the topic exhibit softer rhetoric. These statements are consistent with the evolution of China's engagement with Asian regionalism since the 1990s. They demonstrate that Chinese policy remains focused on engagement with multilateral institutions, even those that appear to cut across China's objectives, or those that China has to work hard to join. It also suggests that China is prepared—perhaps reluctantly—to give space to Asia Pacific institutions and not try to insist that regionalism should be contained within East Asia. It also offers opportunities for the Chinese government to push forward domestic reforms in order to stay competitive and move the Chinese economy to a new level.

Xi Jinping's comment about avoiding a "spaghetti bowl" suggests that China may share a long-term vision of a single broad Asia Pacific free trade arrangement, which could incorporate RCEP, the TPP, and other institutions. In the meantime, for Chinese policymakers it would be preferable for the TPP to become just one more noodle in the bowl than a dominant regional institution of which China is not a member.

Notes

1. I take a constructivist perspective that treats regions as "socially constructed areas defined by state, supra-state, and societal agents, with shifting territorial, economic and socio-political parameters" (Selden 2012).

2. APEC's founding members were Australia, Brunei Darussalam, Canada, Indonesia, Japan, South Korea, Malaysia, New Zealand, the Philippines, Singapore, Thailand, and the United States. The People's Republic of China, Hong Kong, and Chinese Taipei (Taiwan) joined in 1991, followed by Mexico and Papua New Guinea in 1993, Chile in 1994, and Peru, Russia, and Vietnam in 1998, taking full membership to twenty-one.

3. There are some exceptions, such as the Bangladesh-China-India-Myanmar Forum, which I explore in my book *Yunnan: A Chinese Bridgehead to Asia* (Summers 2013: chap. 5).

4. While Chinese foreign policymakers use "East Asia" and other common regional categories, there is also a strong emphasis on the "neighborhood" or "periphery" (*zhoubian*), evident in the high-level internal October 2013 meeting on "neighborhood diplomacy," chaired in Beijing by President Xi Jinping.

5. Some recent official statements have nevertheless referred to "regional integration" (*quyu yitihua*), for example Xi Jinping's 2013 speech to APEC (Xi 2013).

6. Irrespective of China's varying degrees of support for different initiatives, ASEAN is currently developing a stronger institutional identity, gradually advancing toward an ASEAN Community as envisioned by the ninth ASEAN summit in 2003.

7. China is not a member of several institutions covering South and Central Asia, as well as some in Southeast Asia, such as the Mekong River Commission. However, none of these agreements carries the geographic, economic, and strategic significance of the TPP.

7

Toward Consensus on Asia Pacific Financial Stability

Kevin P. Gallagher

THE TRANS-PACIFIC PARTNERSHIP (TPP) AGREEMENT AIMS NOT ONLY TO integrate trade between the numerous countries involved, but also to integrate their financial systems. In the wake of the global financial crisis it is important to ensure that participating TPP nations have the necessary tools at their disposal to prevent and mitigate future crises. In this chapter I argue that recent trade and investment treaties advanced by the United States do not leave ample room for the regulation of cross-border financial flows or the restructuring of sovereign debts. These gaps will have to be addressed in order to formulate a comprehensive twenty-first-century agreement of the sort proposed by the TPP.

Throughout the TPP negotiations, Chile and Malaysia were especially concerned about the deal's implications for financial stability. Chile is renown for deploying cross-border financial regulations on the inflow of speculative capital to a degree that helped it avoid the worst of the crises that swept Latin America in the 1990s. Similarly, Malaysia is credited for being among the least hard-hit during the Asian financial crisis in the late 1990s because it regulated the outflow of capital. In their foreign agreements both countries have pushed hard to include financial safeguards: Chile's deals with Canada and the European Union (though not with the United States) protect its right to regulate financial flows, and Malaysia has achieved similar protection in the World Trade Organization (WTO) and several of its free trade agreements (FTAs). Both countries stood firm on this issue in the TPP and ultimately prevailed.

The TPP's inclusion of financial regulation as a legitimate mechanism for averting instability results not only from pressure by Chile and Malaysia, but also from long-standing support for this position among some members of the US Congress. Congresspersons Barney Frank (author of the Dodd-Frank bill) and Maxine Waters put considerable effort into this issue in the 1990s to ensure that the International Monetary Fund (IMF) granted nations the flexibility to regulate capital flows. In 2003, Frank held hearings at the House Financial Services Committee in support of Chile's efforts to include a safeguard in the US-Chile treaty. Prominent economists and members of think tanks such as Jagdish Bhagwhati, Joseph Stiglitz, and Nancy Birdsall all testified on behalf of the Chilean position. The Office of the US Trade Representative (USTR) and the George W. Bush administration ultimately rejected their argument.

After the 2008 financial crisis and the subsequent passage of the Dodd-Frank bill, Frank teamed with Congressman Sander Levin to pressure the USTR to improve on the errors of past treaties in the TPP. Both offices, as well as the office of Maxine Waters, held numerous meetings with USTR and Treasury officials, arguing that the TPP needed a safeguard that would allow parties to the agreement to regulate financial flows to prevent and mitigate financial crises. In addition to their efforts, over a hundred economists from the United States and other TPP countries signed a letter urging the Barack Obama administration to rectify the TPP in this regard.

The United States remained steadfast against including such provisions until late 2014 and early 2015, when it became clear that Chile and Malaysia would no longer accept no for an answer. The prospect of regional integration under the TPP therefore faced a serious setback. Levin and Frank's offices in the US Congress wrote another set of letters that were endorsed by powerful committee heads. As discussed later, the IMF had also recently ruled that financial regulations should be "part of the toolkit" and had even required that Iceland include such measures as part of its IMF rescue package. The United States ultimately decided that it would approve the TPP's inclusion of both a balance-of-payments exception that permits regulation of capital outflows to mitigate crises and a special annex enabling Chile to deploy its policies on capital inflows.

I aim in this chapter to demonstrate why the capacity of governments to regulate cross-border financial flows is critical for the protection of economic stability. I first examine how existing US agreements have typically denied policy space for financial regulation. I then consider a similar lack of flexibility for sovereign debt restructuring. Finally, I propose some simple steps toward upgrading US approaches to financial regulation, and I argue that the TPP offers an opportunity to improve on past practice. Such improvements are necessary, I conclude, for the TPP to provide a pathway toward consensus and regional integration.

US Trade Policy and the Regulation of Cross-Border Finance

Capital flows—cross-border financial investments that are not foreign direct investment—can be essential parts of government, banking, and corporate finance. Indeed, many developing countries lack the savings or financial institutions to fund business activity and seek capital from abroad to fill the gap. Therefore, under normal circumstances, the more capital flowing into a developing country, the more the country benefits. However, cross-border capital flows tend to be "pro-cyclical": too much money flows in when times are good, and too much flows out during a downturn.

A key characteristic of the global financial crisis has been major swings in capital flows across the globe. With international investment positions now surpassing global output, developing and emerging markets are no strangers to these flows. When the crisis hit, capital rapidly left the developing world in a flight to the "safety" of the US market. In an attempt to recover, many industrialized nations, including the United States, have resorted to loose monetary policy with characteristically low interest rates. Relatively higher interest rates in less industrialized countries, coupled with their strong recoveries driven by Chinese demand for commodities, have triggered yet another surge in capital flows to the developing world. The result has been an increasing concern over currency appreciation, asset bubbles, and inflation.

Under these circumstances, regulations on cross-border financial transactions can help smooth the inflows and outflows of capital and protect developing economies. Most existing regulations target short-term capital flows, typically used for speculative purposes. For example, Colombia's 2007 regulations required foreign investors to park a percentage of their investment in the central bank, which enabled Colombia to avoid some of the outflow losses associated with the global financial crisis (Coelho and Gallagher 2013). Chile and Malaysia, as noted, regulated capital flows in the 1990s to avoid the worst of the damages during crises in that decade (Magud and Reinhart 2006). A recent IMF study found that such regulations have helped developing nations stem currency appreciation and asset bubbles. The study also found that capital controls helped several developing countries buffer the worst effects of the global financial crisis. These findings have led the IMF to endorse the use of capital account regulations as a part of the macroeconomic policy toolkit (Ostry et al. 2010).

Unlike the treaties formulated by most industrialized nations, the template for US trade and investment treaties does not leave adequate flexibility for partner nations to regulate capital flows to prevent and mitigate financial crises. US treaties do not include the regulation of capital flows, since at their core they deem restrictions on the movement of speculative capital as a violation of their terms (Gallagher 2011; Gallagher and Stanley 2012, 2013). As such, they treat regulations of cross-border financial transactions as actionable measures that can trigger investor-state claims. The transfer provisions in the investment chapters of US trade treaties, or in stand-alone bilateral investment treaties (BITs), require that capital be allowed to flow between trading partners "freely and without delay." This position is reinforced in chapters on financial services that usually restrict nations from imposing "limitations on the total value of transactions or assets in the form of numerical quotas" across borders (US Department of State 2010).

In the financial services chapters of US trade treaties and BITs, there is usually a section dedicated to exceptions. Typically included in this section is the "prudential exception," as exhibited in this excerpt from the US-Peru trade treaty:

> 1. Notwithstanding any other provision of this Chapter or Chapter Ten (Investment), Fourteen (Telecommunications), or Fifteen (Electronic Commerce), including specifically Articles 14.16 (Relationship to Other Chapters) and 11.1 (Scope and Coverage) with respect to the supply of financial services in the territory of a Party by a covered investment, a Party shall not be prevented from adopting or maintaining measures for prudential reasons, including for the protection of investors, depositors, policy holders, or persons to whom a fiduciary duty is owed by a financial institution or cross-border financial service supplier, or to ensure the integrity and stability of the financial system. Where such measures do not conform with the provisions of this Agreement referred to in this paragraph, they shall not be used as a means of avoiding the Party's commitments or obligations under such provisions. (Financial Services chapter, Article 12.10.1)

Although the language seems to grant a degree of flexibility in financial sector regulations, capital account regulation is not permissible under this exception. This was confirmed by the USTR and in the 2003 testimony of the undersecretary of treasury for international affairs to the US Congress (Taylor 2003). In practice, the term "prudential reasons" is usually interpreted in a narrow fashion, pertaining to individual financial institutions. Concern has also been expressed in congressional testimony that the last sentence is "self-canceling," effectively belying the measures that seem to be endorsed in the preceding text.

The prudential exception in services chapters or BITs is usually followed by an exception for monetary policy, evident again in the US-Peru trade treaty:

> Nothing in this Chapter or Chapter Ten (Investment), Fourteen (Telecommunications), or Fifteen (Electronic Commerce), including specifically Articles 14.16 (Relationship to Other Chapters) and 11.1 (Scope and Coverage) with respect to the supply of financial services in the territory of a Party by a covered investment, applies to non-discriminatory measures of general application taken by any public entity in pursuit of monetary and related credit or exchange rate policies. This paragraph shall not affect a Party's obligations under Article 10.9 (Performance Requirements) with respect to measures covered by

> Chapter Ten (Investment) or under Article 10.8 (Transfers) or 11.10 (Transfers and Payments). (Financial Services chapter, Article 12.10.2)

This second exception can be interpreted as granting nations the flexibility to pursue monetary and exchange-rate policies, including capital account regulations, that they determine are in their best interests. Yet the last sentence in the paragraph, once again, specifically excludes transfers. Provisions such as these caused bitter controversy during the negotiation of the US-Chile and US-Singapore trade treaties in the early 2000s.

US trade partners have repeatedly asked for a safeguard that includes capital controls, but the United States almost always denies such requests. In a few instances, such as Chile and Singapore, US negotiators have granted special annexes that allow US trade partners an extended grace period before investor-state claims on capital controls can be filed and that permit limits on damages related to certain types of controls. However, these annexes are inadequate in the wake of the global financial crisis for at least four reasons:

- The annexes still allow for investor-state claims related to capital controls—they just require investors to delay claims for compensation. An investor has to wait one year to file a claim related to capital controls to prevent and mitigate crises, but that claim can be for a measure taken during the cooling-off year. For most developing economies, the very prospect of investor-state cases could discourage the use of potentially beneficial controls.
- Unlike the United States, many nations' treaties allow for capital controls. Indeed, the Canada-Chile FTA, the European Union–Korea FTA, the Japan-Peru BIT, and the Japan-Korea BIT (just to name a few) all grant greater flexibility for capital controls (Anderson 2011; Viterbo 2012). The more restrictive conditions demanded by the United States give incentives for nations to apply controls in a discriminatory manner (applying controls on European Union investors, for example, but not on US investors).
- The IMF has expressed concerns that restrictions on capital controls in US agreements, even those with the special annexes, may conflict with the IMF's authority to recommend capital controls in certain country programs, as they have done in Iceland and several other countries.
- The protracted dispute settlement procedure permitted by the United States in its FTAs with Chile and Singapore (noted earlier) has not become a standard feature of US agreements. It is not in the China-ASEAN Free Trade Area (CAFTA), any US BIT, or the pending US-Korea FTA.

For these reasons the IMF has expressed concern about US treaties, and in late 2012 officially endorsed an "institutional view" on the management of capital flows. Though the IMF will continue to urge countries to eventually liberalize all capital transfers, henceforth the IMF will advise nations, according to their circumstances, to deploy controls on inflows and outflows of capital. The IMF is aware that it may recommend capital controls to nations that do not have the policy space to deploy such instruments because they would be deemed actionable under a trade agreement or investment treaty. This delicate topic has opened a fault line of divergence between the IMF and US investment policy:

> The Fund's proposed institutional view would not (and legally could not) alter members' rights and obligations under other international agreements. Rather, conformity with obligations under other agreements would continue to be determined solely by the existing provisions of those agreements. Thus, for example, even where the proposed Fund institutional view recognizes the use of inflow or outflow capital flow management (CFM) measures as an appropriate policy response, these measures could still violate a member's obligations under other international agreements if those agreements do not have temporary safeguard provisions compatible with the Fund's approach. (IMF 2012a: 42)

A similar conclusion was evident in an IMF board report released the same year:

> The limited flexibility afforded by some bilateral and regional agreements in respect to liberalization obligations may create challenges for the management of capital flows. These challenges should be weighed against the agreements' potential benefits. In particular, such agreements could be a step toward broader liberalization. However, these agreements in many cases do not provide appropriate safeguards or proper sequencing of liberalization, and could thus benefit from reform to include these protections. (IMF 2012b: 8)

Despite the IMF's cautionary words, the United States drew on past treaties to propose similar measures for the TPP. Information on the TPP available in early 2015, available largely through leaked chapter drafts, revealed the omission of balance-of-payments exceptions and a narrow prudential exception that would not permit the use of most capital account regulations. Many TPP nations pushed back, as did members of the US Congress, contributing to the agreement's status as one of the most contentious congressional issues in 2015. Stiff opposition from Chile, Malaysia, and a range of respected economists eventually forced the United States to soften its position.

Sovereign Debt Restructuring

As members of the eurozone have become acutely aware, the lack of an authoritative regime for restructuring sovereign debt is one of the most glaring gaps in the international financial architecture. A de facto regime appears to be emerging under which international investment agreements (IIAs) can serve as a way for disgruntled investors to circumvent debt restructuring. This is evident in the 2011 decision of the International Centre for Settlement of Investment Disputes (ICSID) to grant a bilateral investment treaty jurisdiction over Argentina's post-2001 sovereign debt restructure. This mission creep on the part of IIAs has seen them enter legal territory that they are ill equipped to navigate and that would be better navigated by national governments and international financial and monetary authorities.

If managed appropriately, government borrowing can be (and has been for centuries) an essential ingredient for economic development. However, as we are witnessing in Europe, even when nations maintain a healthy ratio of debt to gross domestic product (GDP), they can still spiral into a debt crisis should they become unable (or unwilling) to service their debt. Contagion from other crises or a rapid drop in investor confidence could prevent creditors from rolling over or increasing loans. Moreover, debt is sometimes denominated in a foreign currency, so when interest rates rise or the value of a nation's currency falls (on its own or relative to its neighbors), the cost of debt servicing can skyrocket.

Nations that cannot repay their debts often pursue a process called sovereign debt restructuring, which enables the renegotiation of contracts between creditors and debtors. Sovereign debt restructuring (also called a "workout") often involves a reduction of the face value of the debt and "swaps," wherein new bonds with lower interest rates and longer maturities are exchanged for the defaulted bonds. Workouts are usually discounted and result in a loss, or "haircut," for bondholders. In the early 2000s the IMF proposed a sovereign debt restructuring mechanism that sought to provide a fair forum for negotiation between bondholders and governments. Among its proposed features were a standstill clause to prevent rapid withdrawal of deposits, a facility to provide short-term financing and to prioritize a debtor nation's debt schedule, and limits on the ability of disgruntled minority bondholders to file lawsuits against debtor nations. The US government and business community swiftly rejected the mechanism.

The United States proposed that instead of the sovereign debt restructuring mechanism, collective action clauses should become the default protocol for managing sovereign debt restructures. Collective action clauses have the following features: a "collective representation" component under which bondholders meet to exchange views on the restructure in question;

a "majority restructuring" component that enables a 75 percent supermajority of bondholders to bind all holders within the same bond issue to the terms of the restructuring; and a "minimum enforcement" component whereby a minimum of 25 percent of bondholders must agree that litigation can be pursued.

Among the weaknesses of collective action clauses is that they do not apply across bond issuances, making it difficult to reach agreement on the whole swath of debt that a defaulting nation would like to swap. In part because of such weaknesses, most eurozone bonds (unlike those covered by US agreements) are not subject to such clauses. Even if they were, restructuring would not be burden free for bondholders, since Europe's International Swaps and Derivatives Association takes precedence over collective action clauses and may choose to pay out insurance instead of permitting capital flight.

Most US international investment agreements cover "any type of asset." Since sovereign debt can be portrayed as a "type of asset," US international investment agreements provide investors opportunities to recover the full value of their bonds. Such a portrayal resonates with a recent ICSID ruling that Argentina's post-2001 debt restructuring falls under the jurisdiction of the Italy-Argentina BIT. When Argentina restructured its debt in 2005, close to 180,000 Argentine bondholders filed a claim under the Italy-Argentina BIT for approximately $4.3 billion. Some of those investors settled in a 2010 restructuring, but there are still approximately 60,000 Italian bondholders seeking upwards of $2 billion from Argentina through the ICSID. In September 2013, a private World Bank tribunal decided by majority that Argentina's bond restructuring does indeed fall under the jurisdiction of the BIT. The case will therefore continue, despite dissent from one of three tribunals that has so far examined the case. The bondholders seeking to recover their investments through the trade treaty are among the few remaining holdouts.

The safeguards and exceptions in many countries' IIAs are sufficient to provide cover for nations to restructure their debt. By contrast, only a handful of US treaties contain an annex addressing sovereign debt restructuring. The only so-called safeguard contained in most US agreements is the "essential security" provision. This provision is in fact the opposite of a safeguard, as it is designed to neutralize claims from recipients of US investment that actions they take during a financial crisis are needed to protect national security. Article 18 of the 2004 US Model BIT contains language that is increasingly being emulated in other treaties, particularly the inclusion of provisions: "to preclude a Party from applying measures that *it considers* necessary for the fulfillment of its obligations with respect to the maintenance or restoration of international peace or security, or the protection of its own essential security interests" (USTR 2004, emphasis added). Drawing on Article 18, there are four IIA provisions that investors can invoke to limit the ability of recipient countries to restructure sovereign debt:

1. *Jurisdiction.* If IIAs are deemed to cover "any kind of asset" then it can be argued that sovereign debt falls under the jurisdiction of a given treaty.
2. *Expropriation.* Sovereign debt restructuring could be seen as an indirect expropriation because a restructuring reduces the value of the sovereign bond.
3. *Fair and equitable treatment.* Insofar as this treatment is seen as protecting investors' legitimate expectations, a bond swap that was not expected during the initial investment period could be portrayed as a violation of this standard.
4. *National treatment.* In some financial circumstances, it may be necessary to treat domestic bondholders differently than foreigners. This, though, could be seen to violate national treatment.

The 2004 US Model BIT does not mention economic crises per se, but "all tribunals that have considered the matter thus far have interpreted the rules broadly enough to include such crises" (Salacuse 2010: 345). Despite this apparent consensus, tribunals differ greatly in their assessments of the gravity of a given nation's financial situation. As noted, two out of three tribunals ruled that Argentina could be held liable for the actions it took to halt its crisis. This divided outcome resulted from diverging assessments of whether or not specific protective measures were appropriate and from opposing views about the legitimacy of "self-judged" risks to national security. As indicated in Article 18, no nation entering into a twenty-first-century IIA should expect that the legitimacy of the measures "it considers necessary" to take on the grounds of national security will be internationally recognized. Whether or not a host nation should possess the authority to determine the seriousness of external threats to its security in a globally integrated financial system is a key question of twenty-first-century economic governance. As discussed later, the TPP raises this question at the multilateral level, and for almost the entirety of its negotiation sought to standardize the view that such assessments should be made by international investors rather than the nations they invest in.

Several recent US treaties provide explicit guidelines for managing sovereign debt restructuring. US trade officials are usually reluctant to include such guidelines, as they argue that such restructuring is sufficiently dealt with by collective action clauses. However, when negotiating partners insist, the United States is sometimes willing to compromise with an annex. For instance, a special annex on sovereign debt restructuring is present in the US-Uruguay BIT and in US free trade agreements with Central America, Chile, Peru, and Colombia. Though the specific text varies across the treaties, these annexes usually prohibit claims against "negotiated debt restructuring" unless an investor holds that a restructuring violates national treatment or most-favored-nation status. Such treaties usually define "negotiated restructuring" as a restructuring wherein 75 percent of the bondholders have consented to a change in payment terms. If an investor files a claim in the event of a restructuring that is not a "negotiated" one, she or he must honor a cooling-off period usually lasting 270 days before a claim may be filed. There is no cooling-off period for a nonnegotiated or negotiated restructuring that violates national treatment or most-favored-nation status.

Sovereign debt restructuring annexes are not standard in US treaties post–North American Free Trade Agreement (NAFTA, which excludes sovereign debt from the definition of investment altogether). Indeed, the agreements between the United States and Australia, South Korea, Morocco, Oman, Panama, and Singapore include bonds and debt as covered investments but do not include annexes for sovereign debt restructuring. Two exceptions are the Central America Free Trade Agreement–Dominican Republic (CAFTA-DR, signed into US law in 2005) and the US-Chile FTA (completed in 2009). Both include sovereign debt restructuring annexes, though with strict conditions. For instance, Annex 10-A of CAFTA specifies that sovereign debt restructuring is subject only to Articles 10.3 (covering national treatment) and 10.4 (covering most-favored-nation status). The cooling-off period typically required of investors in pre-NAFTA treaties does not apply, and there is no mention of "negotiated restructuring" as a prerequisite.

Sovereign debt restructuring annexes constitute recognition among signatory parties that restructuring is a special case, and yet these annexes remain far from adequate for at least four reasons. First, collective action clauses may take precedence, leaving open an avenue for investors to seek claims for restructuring. As in the Argentine case, collective action clauses enable vulture funds and other holdouts to neutralize a restructured bond issue by acquiring a supermajority within the issuance, and furthermore enable a 25 percent minority to litigate and arbitrate. Second, the definition of investment and umbrella clauses allow for investor-state arbitration under treaty obligations regardless of whether the obligations are also covered by domestic law. Third, most restructuring concerns multi-issued bonds and therefore suffers from the aggregation problem described earlier. Again, collective action clauses only apply within a single bond issue, not across multiple issues that are often bundled together in a restructuring. Fourth, and very importantly, economists and international financial institutions have repeatedly concurred that, in contradiction with the national-treatment principle, domestic bondholders and financial institutions sometimes need to be treated differently during a crisis. Prioritizing domestic debt may be a necessary step toward reviving a domestic financial system, providing liquidity, and managing risk during a recovery (Gelpern and Setser 2004: 796).

Had Chile and Malaysia not rallied congressional supporters and noteworthy economists to their cause, the TPP would have sought to implement measures similar to those outlined here to facilitate recovery of investments by bondholders. The fact that this prospect was on the agenda, and very nearly became reality, reflects a gradual movement of regulatory jurisdiction away from international financial institutions and sovereign governments toward private sector tribunals. The former take into account a broad range of economic and political factors, while the latter take into account a much narrower range of commercial factors, such as the content of IIAs and BITs. While the TPP ultimately permitted some safeguards, there is no question that its broader intention was—and in many respects still is—to shift the power of international economic regulation increasingly into the hands of large private investors and away from sovereign governments.

Conclusion

It is in the interest of the United States and its trade partners to preserve adequate policy space to prevent and mitigate financial crises. With respect to the regulation of cross-border financial flows and sovereign debt restructuring, several (potentially overlapping) steps are possible.

On financial flows, some IMF officials have gone so far as to recommend that speculative capital in the form of derivatives and other financial "innovations" be omitted from the definition of investment in treaties (Hagan 2000). Another recent IMF proposal is the inclusion of uniform safeguard clauses in all nations' trade and investment agreements (IMF 2012a). Regarding US treaties in particular, the "exceptions" language could be broadened to explicitly allow parties the flexibility to deploy controls and other measures for the purpose of crisis mitigation. Finally, the resolution of disputes over these matters could be more clearly placed under the jurisdiction of regulators and governments that are equipped to consider a broad range of political and economic factors, rather than private investment tribunals whose purview is inherently narrower.

With respect to sovereign debt restructuring, there are three possible nonexclusive policy remedies that would enable international investment agreements to grant nations the policy space to conduct effective restructures. The first is simply the exclusion of sovereign debt from future investment treaties. This would relegate sovereign debt arbitration to national courts and to international financial bodies. Second, treaties must clarify that mitigating financial crises constitutes "essential security" and that essential security exceptions should therefore cover financial crises. Furthermore, sovereign debt restructuring by host nations should be deemed "self-judging" and of "necessity." Third, and this could pertain to cross-border financial regulation as well, state-to-state dispute resolution for sovereign debt restructuring and crisis-related instances may be more prudent than investor-state arbitration given that governments need to weigh a host of issues in such circumstances. Governments attempt to examine the economy-wide or public welfare effects of crises whereas individual firms rationally look out for their own bottom line. Investor-state negotiation tips the cost-benefit upside down, giving power to the "losers" even when the gains to the "winners" (the larger public and the future of a nation) of an orderly restructuring may far outweigh the costs to the losers.

The global financial crisis has made it all too obvious that granting US trade partners the flexibility to use legitimate policies to prevent and mitigate financial crises is also good for the United States. When trade partners fall into financial crisis, the United States loses export markets and associated jobs. Capital controls can help stabilize exchange rates, which is good for long-term investors and for US exporters and importers. Moreover, when other countries cannot control financial bubbles that drive up currency values, US consumers may be hurt by rising prices on imported goods. We have learned all too well that financial instability in a globalized world can be contagious and counterproductive to the integration agenda.

Advocated most assertively by Chile, Malaysia, and US congresspeople on financial services committees, the TPP's proposed provisions for members to regulate capital flows are a step in the right direction, but they will not ensure financial stability on their own. Supporting the stability cause are several other emerging initiatives, such as revised IMF and Group of 20 (G20) guidelines, the Chiang Mai Initiative, the development of domestic bond markets, the new Basel regulations, and efforts to promote "best practices" through the ASEAN+3 finance ministers' meetings. Ultimately the concession made by the US government to permit a degree of capital-flow regulation in the TPP signifies a growing recognition that financial stability is becoming an international priority because it is critical to multilateral integration.

8

Agricultural Exceptionalism: A Potential TPP Roadblock

Alan Smart and Josephine Smart

AMONG THE MOST CONTENTIOUS PROVISIONS OF THE TRANS-PACIFIC Partnership (TPP) are those involving food and agriculture. For trade representatives in Japan, Canada, and other TPP nations, threats to established agricultural production arrangements are a key concern; meanwhile, for consumers, food safety and security are emotionally loaded issues. The latter anxieties have emerged in the context of recent scandals over tainted food originating from China, most notably the use of the toxic chemical melamine in baby formula, provoking widespread fear and anger throughout the Pacific region. A 2011 survey in Japan found that the top reason for "not having a good image of China" was dissatisfaction with the Chinese government's handling of food safety concerns. This perception is widespread, including within China, prompting consumers to seek food from other sources. Hong Kong is among the many regions and countries that, after decades of declining agricultural production, are now witnessing growing demand for its food exports (Smart and Smart 2012b).

China is not the only country denounced for inadequate food safety regulations. Australia and New Zealand were widely criticized in the early 2000s for dumping "unhealthy" fatty lamb and mutton flaps (belly meat) on South Pacific islands, resulting in import bans in Fiji and Tonga (Gewertz and Errington 2010). Meanwhile, disputes over genetically modified organisms and the use of growth hormones in livestock continue to complicate trade relations between the United States and the European Union, contributing to the demise of the World Trade Organization (WTO) Doha round (Skogstad 2008; Smart and Smart 2012a). Despite the declining size of rich countries' agriculture sectors, Carsten Daugbjerg and Alan Swinbank argue that agriculture is "key to understanding the dynamics of trade rounds in the WTO," because "disputes over farm trade liberalization can thwart the whole WTO process" (2009: 3).

The TPP aims to move beyond the Doha deadlock by providing alternative pathways to trade liberalization. However, a long history of "agricultural exceptionalism" may undermine this objective and potentially thwart the TPP process altogether. Recent food price spikes, due in part to increasing demand for meat in emerging markets, have added heat to global and regional disputes about admissible agricultural products, subsidies, and import controls. The disposition of US, Japanese, Canadian, Australian, and other agriculture representatives to reach consensus on these issues weighed heavily on the success or failure of the broader TPP negotiations, and it may yet prevent ratification of the agreement. Their job is made no easier by citizens' food safety concerns, which have galvanized the determination of advocacy groups and nongovernmental organizations (NGOs) that for numerous reasons are already opposed to the TPP.

It is easy to combine food and agriculture when talking about the politics of trade, but the two harbor important differences. Literature on agriculture generally concentrates on producers, with some recent attention to the relationship of agricultural protection with threats to food safety and public health. Research on food, on the other hand, generally emphasizes consumer interests and attitudes, often framing the key issues in a quite different way.

A Google search for "trans-pacific partnership food" generated 1.62 million results compared to only 634,000 for "trans-pacific partnership agriculture," demonstrating the relative importance of food-related issues to consumers. However, compared to the farm (i.e., agriculture) sector, consumer lobbies are much less organized and exert little political influence. Consequently, accounts of what the TPP might mean for food safety vary dramatically. The US consumer-oriented website Expose the TPP states: "The TPP would require us to allow food imports if the exporting country claims that their safety regime is 'equivalent' to our own, even if it violates the key principles of our food safety laws. These rules would effectively outsource domestic food inspection to other countries." By contrast, the *Japan Times* tends to back the interests of national agriculture producers and has consequently advocated less cumbersome food safety standards. One of its recent editorials argues that Japan's stringent safety standards may yet be "dealt with" through an agreement with the United States if the TPP proves incapable:

> The 12 countries involved in the Trans-Pacific Partnership negotiations are unlikely to ease their individual food safety standards as the subject is not being discussed in the free-trade talks, negotiation sources said Wednesday. While this means Japan can maintain its regulations on food additives and pesticides that are stricter than international standards, easing of such rules could still be dealt with in upcoming rounds of Japan-U.S. bilateral talks to be held in parallel with the TPP negotiations, as Washington has called for simpler regulations. (*Japan Times* 2013)

Japan's policies for protecting the agriculture sector have proven no less divisive as the TPP seeks to diminish trade barriers. The decisive electoral victory of Japan's pro-TPP Liberal Democratic Party (LDP) in July 2013 has not quelled deep domestic divisions over protectionism. As a report from the US National Bureau of Asian Research notes: "Many members [of the LDP] will be reluctant to compromise on tariffs over five categories of products: rice, wheat, beef/pork, sugar, and dairy. . . . At the end of the TPP talks, Japan will likely agree to substantially reduce—but perhaps not eliminate—restrictions protecting most of these sensitive products" (Steffensen 2013: 4). Any significant reduction of agriculture tariffs among TPP members will provoke intense internal disputes over the very same agricultural issues that dogged the Doha round. Despite the TPP's attempts to overcome agricultural exceptionalism, the battle is far from over.

Further complicating the prospect of an integrated food governance regime is the paradox that this very pursuit may lead to disunity. As discussed later, the TPP's insistence on scientific testing to prove that a food product is unsafe (and therefore should not be freely traded) may provoke regional fragmentation as local actors interpret the nature and legitimacy of the science that is used. If the requirement for science is valuable, then, we would ask, why is it not used for other forms of trade?

We argue in the first section of this chapter that international attempts to regulate agricultural production have long been intertwined with the politics of trade. From the nineteenth century Corn Laws to the most recent WTO guidelines, agriculture has provoked disagreements about the benefits and detriments of small farming versus large agribusiness. These diverging models have often brought producer and consumer interests into conflict, not least in relation to the health and safety implications of mass production. In the next section we find that a wide variety of international responses to allegedly unsafe Canadian beef belie any semblance of a coherent system for achieving science-based food safety. Regulatory responses have been conditioned by everything from local electoral politics to regional disputes with neighbors, demonstrating how lawmaking invariably passes through a sieve of national interests. To bring multilateral coherence to these fragmented concerns is a key problem for the TPP. In the final section we consider a more recent pressure on international agriculture governance: the growing investment capacities of Chinese state-owned enterprises (SOEs). Accusations of anticompetitive behavior and a track record of unsafe farming in China are prompting foreign regulatory responses. As these responses come into effect, they will create a global environment more conducive to the TPP, a key goal of which is to limit the international reach of SOEs. We conclude that whether or not the TPP achieves this goal, historically entrenched sensitivities toward the production and consumption of food constitute a minefield of risk in the path of effective reform.

Governance in Motion

Throughout history nations have treated agriculture as exceptional. Imperial Chinese leaders saw food security as central to the preservation of the dynastic system and therefore invested heavily in grain storage and flood protection (Li 2007). In Europe, despite the intellectual and political challenge against agriculture's special status (set forth in the 1846 repeal of Great Britain's protectionist Corn Laws), exceptionalism remained prevalent. This was the case worldwide when the General Agreement on Tariffs and Trade (GATT) was created in 1947 (Irwin 1989), and it remained the case at least until the late 1970s, when agriculture in developed countries operated under what Grace Skogstad calls the "state assistance" paradigm (2008: 43). During this period, intervention was justified on the grounds that agricultural pricing mechanisms were "ineffective in achieving an efficient and productive sector and in assuring adequate and stable incomes for farm producers" (Skogstad 2008: 43).

From the late 1970s, special treatment for agriculture came under renewed criticism from economists in the context of expanding regimes of neoliberal governance. Ideas of comparative advantage, deployed by British industrialists to dismantle the Corn Laws and thereby deflate food prices (and wages), were used to argue that freer trade would benefit poor countries even more than rich ones. This argument was premised on the notion of "agricultural normalism," which presents agricultural markets as "basically stable and capable of providing society's desired outcomes. Imbalances and instability in agricultural markets are the consequences of government intervention" (Daugbjerg and Swinbank 2009: 12).

The state assistance paradigm for agriculture is still internationally powerful, but the trend has been away from it, with at least two proposed alternatives. One is the competitive or market-liberal paradigm, promoted by the United States and the Cairns Group of seventeen agriculture exporters including Canada, Australia, and a variety of less economically developed countries. Although Canada's marketing boards still exist, the Canadian Wheat Board monopoly ended in 2011, and the entry of Canada into the TPP negotiations prompted calls to terminate the remaining boards to facilitate the liberalization of other agriculture subsectors. Signed in 2015, the TPP does not require termination of marketing boards, but Canada has agreed to allow dairy imports from TPP countries equivalent to 3.25 percent of domestic production and up to 2 percent for other supply-managed sectors. Elected in late 2015, the new Canadian federal government has not yet indicated if it will support the TPP.

The other contending framework for agriculture governance is the multifunctionality paradigm, championed by the European Union. Under this regime, state assistance to augment agricultural production is discontinued, but support is maintained for other aspects of the sector, such as provision of environmental goods and services, heritage landscape preservation, rural development, and agri-tourism (Marsden and Sonnino 2005).

One sphere of regulation that has long been exempt from attempts to liberalize agriculture trade is food safety. The emergence of food-related crises and conflicts over the past decade has strengthened this trend and drawn attention to its economic, political, and social implications. Among the recent crises are mad cow disease, SARS, avian flu, swine flu, genetically modified crops, growth hormones in livestock, and tainted pet food and cough syrup. Food raises concerns that are less prevalent for mechanical products because of its inherent association with organic materials that can spread infectious diseases (Smart and Smart 2012c). John Spriggs and Grant Isaac argue that mad cow disease and other biological threats "have been a lightning conductor for change around the world in the attitudes of government, industry and consumers towards food safety. . . . [E]ven countries that had no strong domestic reason to improve their food safety had an international imperative to do so—if they wanted to gain and maintain access to international markets" (2001: v). Food can evoke everything from disgust to nostalgia for traditional lifestyles, emotions that are more visceral, deeply held, and easily mobilized to justify restrictions than is the case for other categories of commodities. Cultural products and healthcare are perhaps the closest competitors for this extent of emotional loading.

The Sanitary and Phytosanitary (SPS) Agreement was adopted by the WTO in 1995 to distinguish between protective and protectionist controls on substances that might transmit infections to humans, animals, or plants. The agreement aims to facilitate protection while impeding protectionism by requiring that controls be nondiscriminatory and based on scientific evidence, a combination of requirements that is unique in WTO regulations. These strict standards to ensure food safety and protect the environment have given rise to two interrelated problems: first, such technically demanding requirements are beyond the capacity of most small agricultural enterprises, and second, the creation of large-scale systems and facilities capable of implementing them can intensify the negative consequences when things go wrong.

Chapter 7 of the TPP agreement is devoted to sanitary and phytosanitary measures. It explicitly is intended to "reinforce and build on the SPS Agreement" (7.2.b) and to "protect human, animal or plant life or health in the territories of the Parties while facilitating and expanding trade" (7.2.a). Any measure implemented by a party to the agreement must not "create unjustified obstacles to trade" (7.2.d), and any SPS measures must be "based on scientific principles" (7.9.1). Such measures therefore conform to international standards (either the SPS Agreement or the Codex Alimentarius), or if nonconforming they must be "based on documented and objective scientific evidence that is rationally related to the measures" (7.9.2). Implementation of these principles will be achieved by the establishment of a committee on sanitary and phytosanitary measures composed of parties' government representatives responsible for SPS matters (7.5.1).

According to political commentator Dara Lind, the TPP departs from the WTO's sanitary and phytosanitary standards because the latter imply that it is "sometimes okay for countries to take a precautionary approach to food safety, but they also say regulations should be based in science. That's created constant haggling over what exactly those terms mean. Most trade agreements simply echo the WTO's language on SPS. The TPP very much does not. Instead, it fully embraces the 'scientific' side of the argument: substances should be safe until proven otherwise" (Lind 2015). The TPP avoids any ambiguity on the need for scientific rationale by insisting that products should be freely traded unless scientifically proven to be harmful, but this determination does not resonate with current practice in European and other regions that take a more precautionary approach.

Infectious disease specialists note that the consolidation and increased scale of agricultural and food-processing activity have been accompanied by greater risks (Kimball 2006: 170). Tim Lang and Michael Heasman, for instance, argue that rapid productivity gains in the 1980s had severe health consequences: "Slack had so cleverly been taken out of the system that if something went wrong, it did so catastrophically, as was seen with the UK's BSE [mad cow disease] (1986–) and Foot and Mouth Disease (2001) outbreaks, and with the numerous food safety scandals from the late 1980s" (2004: 28). Stricter standards, like all policy interventions, can thus generate a variety of unintended consequences, including an emphasis on mass production and resulting vulnerability to disease and contamination.

As well as its potential health implications, large-scale production raises a competitive obstacle for small enterprises, particularly in less wealthy nations. Paradoxically, the largest agribusinesses often argue against state intervention in general, but over the long term tighter regulations tend to serve their interests (Freidberg 2004: 220). Indeed, the high cost of adopting increasingly stringent international standards takes a disproportionate toll on least-developed countries (LDCs), whose ability to influence the rules of the game are further diminished by the complicated nature of global agri-food governance institutions (Busch 2004). Moreover, the ability of LDCs to cooperate in resisting agricultural governance initiatives sponsored by rich countries is constrained by divided interests. Agricultural export powerhouses such as Argentina and Brazil harbor different goals to nations with large agricultural populations that produce primarily for domestic consumption, such as India (Weis 2007).

There is no necessary link between agricultural trade promotion and food safety risks. However, in the wake of the UK mad cow disease scandal, critics argued that bringing responsibility for food safety regulation into the trade-oriented Ministry of Agriculture, Fisheries, and Food compromised consumer interests. The resulting recommendation from an internal inquiry into the scandal, of an arm's-length food safety regulator, was accepted on the basis that commercial and health interests do not always align. A similar shift occurred in Canada with the formation of the Canadian Food Inspection Agency in 1997 (Smart and Smart 2009). The agency was created at a time of growing concern about the risks inherent in ascribing regulatory oversight to an institution that benefits from the commercial growth of the industry it is overseeing. An acute conflict of interests became evident in the regrettable comments of Alberta's premier at the time of the mad cow disease outbreak: a sensible farmer, he said, would have known to "shoot, shovel and shut up" (Henton 2013).

One consequence of recent food safety scandals is the emergence of a consumer-oriented food politics, distinct from producer-oriented farm politics, in disputes around trading regimes (Lang and Heasman 2004). This has occurred simultaneously with a shift of governmental energies toward regional and inter-regional trade agreements, stimulated by the difficulty of achieving consensus at the WTO (Duina 2006). The TPP is an ambitious proposal for such an agreement, with immense potential to affect the character and intensity of cross-Pacific agriculture relations. It is logical, then, that consumer and producer priorities will interact in new ways if the TPP comes into effect. The TPP's push for free trade is likely to come into deeper conflict with popular concerns about the quality of food and the loss of traditional agricultural lifestyles.

The TPP and other twenty-first-century multilateral initiatives are evoking new tensions between farmers and urban consumers. It was widely speculated that Canada might have to abandon its agricultural marketing boards in order to achieve a deal. While this outcome was avoided, presumably through strenuous negotiation, the United States has repeatedly—but unsuccessfully—challenged Canada's agricultural marketing system at the WTO and under North American Free Trade Agreement (NAFTA) dispute resolution procedures. The dismantling of the system would hurt those farmers protected by quotas, but reduce consumer prices (at least initially) and give more freedom to transnational agri-food corporations. The former Conservative government was not fundamentally supportive of the marketing boards, expending considerable effort to end the Canadian Wheat

Board's monopoly over the marketing of western Canadian wheat and barley. But the political risks of regulatory liberalization under the TPP are considerable in rural constituencies that tend to vote Conservative.

Japan's entry into the TPP raised the risk of making fundamental agricultural reforms less achievable, given the central position of Japanese farmers in political coalitions. Aware that 1.15 million of Japan's 2.5 million farm households rely on rice farming, Prime Minister Shinzo Abe took on the political risk and made a variety of concessions on agricultural imports. However, an analysis by the agriculture ministry reported that the impact of TPP reforms for twenty-one agricultural items would be "largely limited" and rice imports were "unlikely to increase" (Jiji 2015). Japan's agricultural concessions in the TPP cut deeper than in any other of its free trade agreements (FTAs) but were still less severe than those agreed by other participating countries. As Aurelia Mulgan (2015) writes:

> Tariffs will be abolished on 30 percent of imports in the so-called five "sensitive" categories (rice, wheat and barley, beef and pork, dairy products, and sugar). But for some of these products the measures that will be implemented fall short of full liberalization. The Japan Agricultural Cooperative (JA) organisation has gone on the offensive, saying that "farmers will face tougher competition with major exporters such as the United States; and that great concern and anger are spreading at the grassroots."

While Japan's debate about the risks and benefits of the TPP has focused on conventional disputes over tariffs, a broader controversy is emerging about the deeply political nature of supposedly "science-based" agriculture regulations. As noted earlier, the TPP demands that food products should be freely traded unless scientifically proven harmful. But as the next section demonstrates, through a case study of Canadian beef, vested interests determine the scope and applicability of scientific evaluation. In a world that is localizing as it globalizes, the TPP will struggle to build unity and consensus around the politics of food safety.

Beef, Mad Cow Disease, and the Politics of Food Safety

Canada's experience with bans on its beef exports suggests that commercial decisionmaking does not respond in a uniform way to consumer concerns about food safety. The unique insistence in the agri-food sector that import restrictions be "science-based" might appear to result in a high level of convergence in international standards and sectoral organization. However, the discipline intended by scientific requirements has generated widespread controversy about the nature and legitimacy of the science that is being used. At the national level, political and economic power appears to condition import restrictions at least as much as scientific evidence.

There has been considerable variation in the treatment of Canadian beef by Hong Kong, Taiwan, China, and South Korea. Consumer concerns about food safety are not the main, and certainly not the sole, determinant of these patterns. Hong Kong consumers are just as concerned about food security as South Koreans, but Hong Kong citizens have focused their restrictions almost entirely on contaminated food products imported from the Chinese mainland, while remaining open to Canadian beef. Meanwhile, South Korea has imposed restrictions on Canadian beef because of strong support for domestic beef producers. This support has its own political history, premised on strong reactions against the efforts of the United States to promote the reopening of South Korea to US beef in the US–South Korea FTA.

Demonstrations of up to half a million people in 2008 prompted offers of resignation from the entire Korean cabinet and created a situation in which politicians came to dread the risks of permitting the entry of Canadian beef. A comparable situation occurred in Taiwan, where a rapid opening to US beef prompted a negative public reaction, and subsequently delayed the opening of markets for Canadian beef. While US bilateral relations with South Korea and Taiwan have clearly impacted both nations' foreign trade policies, China's reluctance to readmit North American beef is harder to explain and may result, in part, from the rapid growth of Chinese cattle production.

These examples demonstrate that global agriculture governance continues to be transmuted through the sieve of local politics and national interests, resulting in a wide variety of regulatory systems. This diversity is further broadened by the ability of producers to evade, resist, and reinterpret national regulations, producing considerable subnational variation in the rules of the game. Just as consumers have come to desire a "relocalization" of their food supply, producers have come to "relocalize" prevailing regulations, even while their national agencies attempt to control and verify their production practices.

Discerning the true motivations of governments is perhaps best left to historians with subsequent access to declassified documents. The obstacles posed to researchers of sensitive, present-day issues such as food safety are especially acute in countries whose governments are not bound to freedom-of-information and transparency legislation. Nevertheless, comparing East Asian instances of closings and reopenings to food imports—in this case Canadian beef—makes it clear that decisions are driven by more than scientific evidence. Science rarely determines the timing, extent, and duration of import bans and reopenings, despite WTO requirements that it should (Noiville 2006).

Their emotional and visceral nature has made food production and consumption highly contentious activities to regulate. This is evident in the stalled Doha round and is likely to become increasingly evident in the TPP negotiations. As noted earlier, fundamental conflicts of interest between food producers and consumers, with the latter beginning to encroach on the traditional producer-dominance in agricultural trade politics, make acceptable national compromises very difficult to achieve. These political difficulties at the national level in turn create barriers to regional and global conclusions to trade negotiations.

These dynamics are evident in the WTO's 2013 Bali trade facilitation agreement. India stalled the agreement's progress on the basis of its food security law, which pledges $4 billion per year to provide cheap food to 800 million people and guarantee minimum support prices for farmers. While the Indian government "insists it will not sacrifice food security on the altar of a trade deal," studies show that the Bali agreement could boost developing country gross domestic product (GDP) by $523 billion and create 21 million jobs, particularly for India (*The Economist* 2014: 58). When trade liberalization is presented as a threat to food security, nationalist politicians can draw on powerful emotions and commitments by promoting populist policies, even if empirically the policies may end up benefiting noncompetitive producers more than poor consumers. Food health and safety concerns are often bound up with critiques of large-scale agribusiness at home and abroad and are often mobilized in the service of protectionism. For this reason, disagreements over agriculture will likely slow the TPP's ratification and have already generated compromises that substantially reduce the breadth and depth of its liberalization agenda.

While the United States is generally in favor of trade liberalization, its sugar lobby was extremely effective in minimizing the TPP's impact on sugar imports, leaving Australian exporters dissatisfied. The US sugar program includes a price-support level for raw cane sugar of 22.25 cents per pound at a time when global raw sugar prices are around 12 cents. Speaking about the TPP's potential relevance for sugar on 1 July 2015, US trade representative Michael Froman said, "Whatever we do in that area won't undermine the sugar program" (Pearson 2015). The modest liberalization offered by the United States in this sector substantiated Froman's claim.

If the politics of food production and consumption condition the flow of agricultural trade, it dominates the flow of agricultural investment. The next section considers how the growing international influence of Chinese state-owned enterprises may be stimulating new approaches to the regulation of inbound agricultural investment. Alongside nationalist sensitivities, emotional concerns over food security and safety are exerting substantial influence over emerging frameworks for the globalization of agriculture.

Outward Agricultural Investment by Chinese State-Owned Enterprises

Nowhere is demand for food expanding so rapidly as China, provoking Beijing to pursue international strategies to achieve national food security. China's rise has been characterized not only by the growth of its population and urbanization, but also by its evolution from being almost exclusively a recipient of foreign investment to an increasingly important outward investor. China's outward foreign investment (OFI) reached $101 billion in 2013, increasing from $88 billion in 2012, making it the third largest source in the world (UNCTAD 2014: xv). These figures do not include the Special Administrative Region of Hong Kong, which by itself is the fifth largest source of OFI, with a total of $92 billion in 2013 (UNCTAD 2014: 7).

Chinese OFI in agriculture has grown considerably in recent years, including in developed countries. Chinese firms were involved in the near wholesale purchase of the dairy sector in New Zealand (Adams 2012; Gray 2013), the 240,000-acre Cubbie Station in Australia in 2012 (Coory 2012), and the acquisition of the largest US pork producer, Smithfield Foods, in September 2013. These investments have incited public debates about the relative merits of short-term economic gains versus long-term national strategic interests (de la Merced 2013; Pierson 2013). Meanwhile, Chinese agriculture investments in Africa, Southeast Asia, and Latin America have attracted negative attention premised on local perceptions of land grabs and diminished local food security (Hearn 2012, 2013a; Sautman and Yan 2007, 2008, 2009; Yan and Sautman 2010).

A common theme in debates about Chinese foreign investment in food and agriculture is that ownership by Chinese SOEs may negatively impact local food production and distribution systems, food safety standards, and ecological sustainability. These debates focus on the general risks to food safety posed by globalization (Ellefson, Zach, and Sullivan 2013; Patel 2008; Morgan, Marsden, and Murdoch 2006; Weis 2007), the poor record of China in protecting the public from toxic food and unethical/unsafe farming practices (Barboza 2008; *The Economist* 2011; Gale and Buzby 2009), and the vulnerability of local food production systems and ecologies to policy changes (Ghitter and Smart 2009; Larsen 2005; Muller 2008; Peine and McMichael 2005; Skogstad 2008).

In the case of Canada, enterprises from the United States, the Netherlands, and elsewhere have made significant investments in agriculture without creating the kind of public controversy associated with Chinese investment. Greater sensitivity toward the entry of Chinese finance may have less to do with China per se than a domestic reawakening of broader concerns about the perceived loss of control over natural resources. These concerns hark back to the 1970s, when homegrown corporations faced intense competition from US counterparts. Fears of economic domination by foreign multinationals are therefore long-standing, predicated on a preoccupation with becoming a "branch-plant economy" whose managers make decisions in the interests of foreign head offices (Clement 1983; Watkins 1985).

Anxiety about excessive foreign influence in agriculture became prominent during the debates about the Canada-US Trade Agreement and NAFTA. The 1988 federal election was fought mostly on the NAFTA issue, and 57 percent of the electorate voted for the two opposition parties that portrayed the agreement as "selling out Canada to the Yanks" (Baughn and Yaprak 1996: 762). The Canadian public also expressed widespread opposition to the free market-oriented Multilateral Agreement on Investment of the Organization for Economic Cooperation and Development (OECD), which was announced in 1997 only to collapse a year later (Jackson and Sanger 1998).

Foreign direct investment in Canada is governed by the Investment Canada Act, which was adopted by the new Conservative government in 1985. The act allows the federal government to forbid foreign investments of significant size if they do not present a "net benefit to Canada." By 2013 the definition of "significant" had grown to $344 million, bearing out the act's long-standing intention to further open Canada to foreign investment. Among the act's reforms was to narrow the scope of the Foreign Investment Review Agency (FIRA), which was renamed Investment Canada. FIRA had been set up by Pierre Trudeau's Liberal government to limit increasing US ownership of Canadian business (Myers and Myers 1985).

The United States has long been the primary referent of Canadian economic nationalism, but China has begun to provoke comparable reactions. Critics emphasize the government subsidies and low-interest loans afforded Chinese competitors, the lack of reciprocity in Chinese treatment of Canadian companies, and the unfair playing field that results. The reluctant approval of China National Offshore Oil Corporation's C$15 billion takeover of Nexen in 2012 provoked intense public debates, as well as calls for a more explicit and sophisticated policy for regulating foreign ownership of key natural resources. The episode revealed perceptions that competition between private firms and subsidized foreign SOEs is unfair. Such perceptions are likely to deepen as Chinese SOEs expand their international interests, especially in agriculture, a sector tightly bound up in concerns about the safety of food production and consumption.

The Canadian government appears to be aware of these intensifying concerns, recently issuing a press release that offers some clarification of its foreign investment policy:

> The burden of proof is on foreign investors to satisfy the Minister [of Industry] that a particular investment is likely to be of net benefit to

> Canada. Investments by foreign SOEs to acquire control of a Canadian oil sands business will, going forward, be found to be of net benefit on an exceptional basis only. The Minister will also continue to carefully monitor SOE transactions throughout the Canadian economy. In particular, the Minister will closely examine: the degree of control or influence a state-owned enterprise would likely exert on the Canadian business that is being acquired; the degree of control or influence a state-owned enterprise would likely exert on the industry in which the Canadian business operates; and the extent to which a foreign state is likely to exercise control or influence over the state-owned enterprise acquiring the Canadian business. Non-controlling minority interests in Canadian businesses proposed by foreign SOEs, including joint ventures, will continue to be welcome in the development of Canada's economy. (Government of Canada 2012)

Although the statement emphasizes oil sands, it positions the Canadian government to tighten control over other sectors of interest to foreign SOEs, including agricultural production and food sales. It therefore permits greater scope for dealing with large Chinese investors on Canadian terms. Critically, this orientation aligns with the TPP's ambition to craft emerging structures of global governance that among other things limit the international reach of SOEs.

China is not party to the TPP negotiations, but as several of the chapters in this volume show, its interests would be affected by TPP stipulations. Most observers believe that the TPP is not just a deal between the current negotiating partners, but also an attempt to set the ground rules for future trading arrangements in a region—and world—in which China's influence is rising (Steffensen 2013; Fergusson et al. 2013). For William Krist of the Woodrow Wilson Center, the TPP negotiations "represent the best opportunity at this time for developing trade rules for the 21st century—rules that will restrict the ability of countries to distort the trade system to their own advantage at the expense of their trade partners" (2012: 24). A key purpose of such rules, Krist argues, is to more effectively restrict the behavior of SOEs (2012: 17). In a world of intensifying concerns about anticompetitive investment from foreign SOEs, and uncertainty about the impact of such investments on food production and consumption, the TPP appears to have China in its sights.

Conclusion

The TPP's ambitious attempt to liberalize regional and global trade through the reform of established "protectionist" arrangements faces acute political risks. Issues of national sovereignty are inevitably sensitive, particularly those that affect the livelihood and health of citizens. Agriculture is at the forefront of this quandary: political risk largely exempted it from liberalization under the GATT, and has considerably slowed its reform under the WTO. The perpetual deferral of reform has, paradoxically, entrenched institutional practices that further reduce the prospects for change. A key question for the TPP is whether or not it will cultivate a fresh line of regulatory evolution.

The release of the final TPP text in October 2015 suggests that the negotiating parties have largely accepted the political risks, though these risks have been tempered with lukewarm reforms in politically sensitive sectors such as sugar in the United States, rice in Japan, and dairy in Canada. Whether or not the TPP nations will be able to ratify the agreement remains uncertain, even in the United States, where it holds strategic implications for US leadership of global economic affairs. A congressional decision not to approve the TPP would dramatically reduce the level of confidence that TPP members have in US leadership.

Also uncertain is whether Canada's new Liberal government will support the TPP or attempt to reopen negotiations on one or more of its clauses. The TPP was a significant issue in the October 2015 election, which saw the demise of Stephen Harper's Conservative government. The New Democratic Party stated that it would not sign the TPP before having seen the text, and current prime minister Justin Trudeau stated during the election that his Liberal Party would not decide on the agreement until he too saw the text. The text was not released when TPP negotiations concluded on 5 October, but only after the Canadian election, and Trudeau has still not made a statement on the government's position. The Liberal Party has been less supportive of closer ties with the United States than its Conservative opponent, under whose government both the Canada–United States Free Trade Agreement and the North American Free Trade Agreement were negotiated and ratified.

Against the backdrop of Canada's political evolution, recent food safety scandals have galvanized global consumers and generated pressure for change in unexpected ways. Citizens around the world are concerned about the potentially negative impact of trade liberalization on food production, safety, and security. On the one hand this is generating further resistance to market-oriented reforms, but on the other it is advancing a call for new regulatory approaches. Existing agricultural protections are widely perceived as incapable of safeguarding fundamental food safety values and, as noted, stricter protections may even be at odds with these values when they encourage large-scale industrial agriculture. The attitude of many food activists might be summarized as "a pox on all your houses," with neither domestic nor transnational corporations trusted to prioritize food safety, national food security, and international "food sovereignty."

Even as they seek new pathways to trade liberalization, governments are wary that deregulation could open opportunities to anticompetitive state-owned enterprises. The TPP explicitly seeks to limit the activities of SOEs in its bid to create a "level playing field" of private enterprise. At a time when Chinese SOEs are increasingly "going out" to invest overseas, the TPP poses risks to them that the Chinese government presumably takes seriously and will try to counteract (see Chapter 9). This is especially the case in international agriculture, which Chinese SOEs are investing in like never before to ensure their nation's food security and safety. As they advance their global quest for stable and safe sources of food, Chinese SOEs therefore stand in the crossfire of two emerging pressures: anxiety about the encroachment of foreign SOEs on national land and concerns about the safety of their large-scale operations.

The new politics of food safety, combined with the old politics of agricultural protection, constitutes a minefield of political risk standing in the path of reform. The TPP and other "mega-regional" agreements may offer a glimmer of hope—and possibly even an easy way out—for reform-oriented governments, which can blame unpopular policy choices on the demands of negotiating partners, or characterize these choices as the tradeoffs necessary for achieving more broadly beneficial national goals. The Japanese government has adopted this strategy in the TPP, though the disposition of its citizens to accept potentially damaging reforms is still by no means certain.

Similarly uncertain is the broader impact that the TPP will have on the transpacific integration of food and agriculture governance. The deal may achieve a degree of unity under the banner of science that would not have been possible in a negotiating arena that included European nations, and it may influence European approaches should it come into force. Also possible, though, is a return to "reform deferral," especially if TPP governments come to the same conclusion as their GATT and WTO predecessors: that agriculture is simply too difficult to deregulate.

9

Adapting to the TPP: Chinese Investment in Overseas Agriculture

Adrian H. Hearn

IN HIS STATEMENT TO THE CHINA DEVELOPMENT FORUM IN MARCH 2013, Prime Minister Li Keqiang reiterated a key commitment of the twelfth Five-Year Plan: instead of depending on exports to generate growth, "we have to rely on domestic consumption" driven by urbanization (*Global Times* 2013b). To achieve this, he said on another occasion, will require China to import some $10 trillion worth of commodities by 2018 and invest $500 billion overseas (World Economic Forum 2013a).[1] In this chapter I examine how China's ability to secure a key commodity in the urbanization process—food—may be affected by the Trans-Pacific Partnership (TPP). I argue that the TPP, if successfully implemented, will pressure Chinese firms to adjust the way they negotiate with member nations.

As noted in Chapter 8, one of the TPP's implications for China is its prospective restriction of state-owned enterprises (SOEs), whether of signatory nations or of foreign governments investing in them. This proposition goes beyond "competitive neutrality," a policy precept that since the mid-1990s has attempted to impede SOEs from receiving concessions or benefits beyond those of competing private enterprises. Derek Scissors of the Heritage Foundation argues that a central feature of the TPP is its potential to more assertively limit the reach of SOEs through "enhanced" competitive neutrality: "One reason for [the TPP's] importance is that it is intended to set a precedent for treatment of state-owned enterprises. . . . It would be a gaping weakness if the TPP and future agreements did not effectively check SOEs. It is the correct goal to minimize the harm caused by their existence and behavior and, in that light, the ideal solution is simple: SOEs should be banned outright from as many economic activities as possible" (2013b: 4).

Reservations about this aspect of the TPP are strongest in Vietnam, Malaysia, and other signatories in which national SOEs play a prominent economic role. The implications of "enhanced" competitive neutrality are relevant, though, to all TPP countries that receive—or hope to receive—

investment from Chinese government sources. As the Chinese state seeks to buy or rent foreign arable land to sustain domestic urban diets, food-exporting nations could see their agriculture sectors revitalized by an injection of Chinese finance. However, the TPP may complicate the ability of Chinese SOEs and government financial institutions to undertake large-scale, vertically integrated investments in member countries unless they develop countermeasures.

Defining the criteria that constitute an SOE, measuring these criteria against actual cases, and harmonizing a consensual definition across distinct contexts will be no simple task for TPP members. Should the TPP come into force, inevitable local compromises forged during implementation will leave open a series of loopholes for SOEs. Ensuing public debates will be heated, not least because perspectives on the merits and dangers of Chinese investment tend to be polarized and entrenched. This heat, though, will enable a long-overdue airing of concerns that currently simmer below the surface, especially in relation to Chinese investment in land. As Alan and Josephine Smart write in Chapter 8, agriculture is an "emotionally loaded" sector, infused with commitments to territorial sovereignty and cultural sensitivities "that are more visceral, deeply held, and more easily mobilized to justify restrictions than is the case for other categories of commodities."

By contrast to Chinese SOEs, multinational private agriculture firms like Archer Daniels Midlands, Bunge, Cargill, and Louis Dreyfus are likely to see their already significant operations in Australia, Canada, and the United States enhanced by the TPP.[2] The agreement's procurement rules enjoin signatory governments to favor the most competitive investors and providers, such as these, over less competitive national firms. These "Big Four" multinational food producers are therefore set to increase their share of international markets, including China's. While this may ease China's food bottleneck, greater reliance on foreign firms stands at odds with the Chinese government's ambition to diversify suppliers and gradually become more self-sufficient in strategic sectors. For the Chinese state, a preferable pathway to food security is to control the supply chain through greater vertical integration and ownership of foreign agriculture assets, from plantations to freight terminals. The TPP's restrictions on SOEs may frustrate this ambition.

Chinese negotiators are responding to their nation's food security challenges—and the TPP's potential intensification of these—by redoubling their efforts to establish trade agreements with agriculture exporters worldwide. China's enthusiasm for a free trade agreement (FTA) with Latin America's Southern Common Market (Mercosur) is fueled by the prospect of long-term supply of food and other commodities, as is the rising tide of Chinese agriculture investments in Africa and Eastern Europe. Having to choose between TPP and non-TPP countries, though, is becoming less likely as Beijing pursues FTAs that carve out exceptions to TPP restrictions in Australia, Japan, and (proposed member) South Korea. Furthermore, China's largest agriculture SOE, the China National Cereals, Oils, and Foodstuffs Corporation (COFCO), has implemented a foreign merger and acquisition strategy that will enable it to leverage the strengths of subsidiaries around the world.

The chapter draws together these considerations to support my argument that the TPP is influencing how Chinese enterprises invest in signatory nations. The agreement has already pushed the Chinese government to advance its own strategy of regional integration through alternative FTAs, acquisition of established agriculture multinationals, and empowerment of the Chinese private sector to conduct overseas deals. This last process resonates with the TPP's goals, but to expand it may require government subsidies, preferential treatment, and even state ownership of apparently private firms. Underwriting private companies with government finance is inconsistent with the TPP, but this practice forms part of China's approach to integration with market economies.

In light of these dynamics, member nations should assess the merits of the TPP according to their own specific developmental needs. These include upgrading agriculture infrastructure, generating employment, maintaining a competitive environment, and expanding value-adding segments of production chains. Whether funded by public or private capital, Chinese or otherwise, investment proposals should be assessed for these criteria on a case-by-case basis rather than through generalized restrictions on SOEs. The latter course could generate countermeasures from SOEs and government investors that undermine the TPP's credibility as a platform for regional integration.

The chapter first explores how urbanization has put new pressure on the Chinese government to safeguard national food security through greater agricultural self-sufficiency at home and acquisition of arable land overseas. It then examines the risks, benefits, and reactions to Chinese agriculture investments in non-TPP member Brazil and by comparison in TPP member Australia. The third section considers countermeasures at the disposal of Chinese firms to overcome the TPP's proposed limits on SOE activity. I conclude that the Brazilian and Australian cases harbor useful information for TPP members as they debate the agreement's ratification and consider how Chinese investment may serve their development goals.

The Local Roots of Foreign Agriculture

"Tie ban niu rou" (sliced fried beef), exclaimed Mr. Wang as he placed the large glass bowl in the center of the table. For two months I had enjoyed pork, beef, and chicken almost every evening during my stay with Mr. Wang, his wife, and his daughter in the South Beijing suburb of Pu Huang Yu. I had met the family while living nearby six years earlier in 2007, shortly after Mr. Wang had moved into the cramped two-bedroom apartment from a village in Hebei province. Even without the rent I was paying him, Mr. Wang's job as a clerk in the administration office of his residential complex sustained a diet that a decade ago would have been unthinkable.

Like the Wang family, 200 million additional Chinese citizens are expected to leave behind rural agriculture for urban consumer culture by 2020. The National New-Type Urbanization Plan envisions 60 percent of China's projected population of 1.43 billion living in cities by that year (860 million people), up from 54 percent when the plan was unveiled in March 2014 (*Xinhua News* 2014a). Integrally linked to this process is the Chinese government's plan to fuel future economic growth through greater domestic consumption, enabling it to reduce investment's share of gross domestic product (GDP) from around 45 percent to around 25 percent.

Augmenting the number of urban consumers is central to the government's strategy, but the food necessary to sustain them is in short supply. With only 9 percent of the world's arable land, a diminishing base of agricultural producers, and an expanding population of urban consumers, China must develop new strategies for feeding its citizens. The domestic production and foreign acquisition of urban staples like beef, pork, chicken, and grains (particularly animal feed derived from soy) are becoming increasingly important to the viability of the Chinese government's vision of national economic development.

Despite its geographic enormity and relatively successful agricultural reforms, only 11 percent of China's surface is arable, and the average property measures a little over one hectare. Furthermore, due to global warming, deforestation, and a chronic shortage of water, the Gobi Desert in China's northeast has expanded rapidly over the past decade. The Chinese government has invested $7 billion to stop desertification by planting trees, but the Gobi is consuming approximately 1,500 square miles of Chinese grassland each year. The scarcity of land, most of which is in any case low-performance, is a serious problem in light of growing demand for food.

To exercise better control over the production of strategic agricultural resources and diminish exposure to volatile international food prices, the Chinese government is pursuing greater self-sufficiency in meats, grains, and other agriculture products. The challenge is to identify an optimal mix of foreign and domestic inputs, and to gradually build national capacity to augment production of the latter. This tactic is evident in China's plan to increase national grain production capacity by 50 billion kilograms by 2020, formulated by the National Development and Reform Commission

(NDRC). The plan envisions 95 percent coverage of China's grain demand through national production by 2020: "it is imperative to stick to the principle of basically achieving grain self-sufficiency domestically" (GAIN 2010: 2).

China already produces 500 million metric tons of grains per year (including cereals, tubers, and pulses), but demand is projected to reach 572 million metric tons by 2020 (GAIN 2010: 2). To address the shortfall, the NDRC has repeatedly stressed the importance of technical upgrading. Its 2013 report on implementation of the 2012 Plan for National Economic and Social Development notes that projects "for spreading agricultural technology were carried out in nearly all towns and townships," enabling the conservation of the nation's 121 million hectares of arable land, the allocation of 107 million hectares to grain cultivation, and the production of 19 million tons of "policy-supported grain for the year" (NDRC 2013: 2–3). Technical efforts have focused on increasing yield through large-scale irrigation, water conservation, upgraded pumping and drainage stations, and management of rivers to create new reservoirs and prevent floods. An accompanying goal is "to carry out major transgenic species development projects and accelerate research on new transgenic grain species" that are high-yield, resistant to multiple diseases, and tolerant of drought (GAIN 2010: 23).

As well as upgrading domestic agricultural capacity, the Chinese government is confronting its nation's geographic constraints by redoubling efforts to secure sources of overseas supply. The 2013 deal struck by the Xinjiang Production and Construction Corps to buy 3 million hectares for grain and pork production in the Ukraine, while delayed by recent political instability, illustrates the scale of investment that Chinese SOEs are willing and able to execute to advance their government's food security goals. In their quest for overseas resources, they have shown preference for simultaneous acquisition of upstream and downstream segments of production, a process of vertical integration that has given the Chinese government a high degree of control over its international supply chains across numerous sectors (Ellis 2009). "The Chinese government," writes Joshua Kurlantzick, "wants to control the entire process, from taking commodities out of the ground to shipping them back to China, because it does not trust world markets to ensure continuous supplies of key resources" (2008: 200).

A concluded TPP would complicate the ability of Chinese firms to vertically integrate their operations in member nations. Its chapter on investment requires signatories to implement steps toward competitive neutrality for SOEs, whether their own or those of foreign nations operating within their borders. These steps range from limits on assets available for acquisition by SOEs to mandatory partnerships with private sector firms at all stages of the production chain. Such requirements, writes Claude Barfield, "set down a marker for China" by promoting diversification away from members' public sectors (2011: 7). While the TPP seeks to encourage a broader mix of economic actors, it could also impede diversification by requiring governments to indiscriminately award contracts to the most competitive private multinational firms, most of which are headquartered in the United States.

Allegations that Chinese SOEs harbor ulterior motives, from anticompetitive impact on supply and pricing to politically mandated expansion of the Chinese Communist Party's global influence, are difficult to substantiate. Whether their ties to government finance are declared or not, there is no conclusive evidence that Chinese enterprises have pursued or achieved these outcomes. Brazil and Australia, to which we now turn, exhibit similar reservations toward Chinese investment, but the latter's involvement in the TPP brings a new layer of regulatory oversight that could help to address emerging concerns. The focus of this oversight will need to be sharpened, though, if it is to encourage industrial upgrading, value adding, and job creation.

Brazil and Australia: Shared Challenges and Mutual Insights

China became the main trade partner of Brazil and Australia when the global financial crisis weakened US demand for manufactured goods and their component natural resources. Both countries' trade and investment with China have subsequently grown, but the fact that mining and energy constitute 78 percent of Chinese investment in Brazil, and 70 percent in Australia, has engendered antagonism. The annual poll conducted by the Lowy Institute for International Policy (2014) shows that 56 percent of Australians believe their government is allowing too much investment from China. Similarly, a leading Latin American public opinion poll shows that Brazilians are yet to embrace China's growing influence in their country and the wider region (LAPOP 2014).

Australian and Brazilian public figures, industry groups, and media express similar concerns about Chinese investment in their agriculture sectors. These include allegations that the Chinese government provides its enterprises with unfair subsidies, accusations that the Chinese state wishes to "colonize" national territory, and claims that Chinese investment projects lack transparency about state and private ownership (Cranston 2012; *Estadão* 2010). Appeals for calm and introspection about historical racism have also emerged in both countries. In 2014 Brazilian president Dilma Rousseff warned of "absurd xenophobia" toward China, while Australian historian Marilyn Lake (2010) has argued that attitudes toward Chinese investment reflect fears of "yellow peril" accrued over decades.

Despite their shared economic reliance on natural resource exports, Brazil has not climbed value chains and developed robust governance frameworks as successfully as Australia (Eslake 2011). As China occupies a more central economic role in both nations, the two stand to learn from each other about what regulatory approaches work best. Australia's Department of Foreign Affairs and Trade is closely watching the fallout of Brazil's 2010 cap on foreign land acquisition at 5,000 hectares. Conversely, the China-Brazil Business Council is attuned to Australia's progress in developing "legislation and institutions which can clearly distinguish and characterize opportunities and threats arising from the sale of land to foreign groups" (CBBC 2011: 26).

Australian and Brazilian similarities and differences afford opportunities for mutual lessons. As two of the world's leading agriculture exporters, they provide comparative insight into the regulation and management of agribusiness, including how the TPP may affect the entry of Chinese investment. Citizen groups in both countries, with support from political allies, have expressed concerns about the ulterior motivations of Chinese SOEs. Backlashes against Chinese investment nevertheless contrast with government policy. Senior Brazilian and Australian politicians have invited more investment from Chinese SOEs, and in the latter case are facilitating it through legal pathways that circumvent prospective TPP restrictions.

Claiming the Land in Brazil

Concerns about Chinese acquisition of arable land are often expressed through websites, social media, and offhand remarks like that of former Brazilian minister of finance Antônio Delfim Netto that "the Chinese have bought Africa and now they're trying to buy Brazil" (quoted in Powell 2011). Reported in mainstream media, Delfim's comment attracted broad support (e.g., *Estadão* 2010), prompting the federal government to formally revive a national land registry system and introduce a 5,000-hectare (and maximum 25 percent) limit on foreign land investments.[3] Brazilian researchers Rodrigo Maciel and Dani Nedal suggest that this legislation goes beyond the protection of national interests: "Sinophobia has also played a part in recent legislation limiting land purchases by foreign companies and individuals. Chinese FDI [foreign direct investment] is said to be qualitatively different from that of traditional sources because of the controlled and opaque nature of the Chinese economy, China's selectivity in allowing inbound FDI, and the close association between investing companies and the Chinese state" (2011: 250).

Chinese interest in acquiring arable land became a topic of national debate prior to Brazil's 2010 election. Sergio Amaral, chairman of the China-Brazil Business Council, argued that restrictions on Chinese investment were justified because they resemble China's own limits on inbound investment: "The Chinese are selective with the capital they let in. They don't accept every kind of investment. After the election, we should consider if the same shouldn't happen here" (quoted in Wentzel 2010). Benjamin Steinbruch, vice president of the São Paulo State Federation of Industries (FIESP), alleged that the Chinese government was attempting to control Brazilian assets and that this constituted a challenge to national security (Rehder and Friedlander 2010).

These perspectives contrast with the enthusiasm of Brazilian politicians and industry leaders toward Chinese finance during Hu Jintao's monumental 2004 Latin American tour, when international media reported his promise to invest $100 billion in the region by 2010. Eager to publicize the share he had secured for Brazil, President Luiz Inácio Lula da Silva declared that "the awaited $7 billion of Chinese investments in Brazil will help the country to regain its competitiveness in strategic sectors such as infrastructure, energy, steel, and telecommunications" (quoted in Maciel and Nedal 2011: 249). Between 2005 and 2013, Brazil received $31 billion of Chinese investment, making it the fourth largest destination for Chinese finance after the United States, Australia, and Canada, but a decade after Hu's visit this investment remains overwhelmingly focused on energy and metals (Heritage Foundation 2015).

The significance of Lula's declaration was not its misreading of Chinese intentions, but the reflection it provoked about the differences between value-adding and resource-seeking finance. This is a critical distinction for Brazil as the "mining boom" slows and opportunities for higher value-added exports—including in food production—emerge. The growing importance of agriculture to the Brazilian economy does not in itself ensure this transition, as it is driven mainly by exports of raw soybeans to China. In 2013–2014, Brazil produced 88 million tons of soybeans and accounted for 45 percent of China's soy imports. A twofold increase in the price of soybeans in 2013 (to $534 per ton) saw the expansion of Brazil's soy plantations to 28 million hectares (a 10 percent increase from 2012) (IMF 2014). A slump in 2014 to $372 per ton, brought on largely by increased production in the United States, has reinforced this upward geographic trend as producers try to compensate for lower returns with greater volume. The cumulative result, say the critics, is overdependence on China.

Notions of dependency have deep historical roots in Brazil, whose earlier status as a Portuguese colony and later relations with the United States entrenched a disadvantageous pattern of cheap commodity exports in return for expensive manufactured imports. The need to escape from this value-eroding predicament was the thrust of Raúl Prebisch's seminal 1950 book *The Economic Development of Latin America and Its Principal Problems,* which led Brazil and most of its neighbors to pursue import substitution industrialization from the 1950s until the 1980s.

The continuing influence of dependency theory on governance in Brazil is evident in broad academic and executive consensus that the state should be entrusted to manage economic affairs and impose strict limits on foreign investment (e.g., Cardoso 2001; Cardoso and Faletto 1979; Oliveira 2006). In some respects, support for state economic stewardship has facilitated Sino-Brazilian "South-South cooperation" with China through large government-led energy, mining, and agriculture initiatives and the New Development Bank of the BRICS bloc (Brazil, Russia, India, China, and South Africa) (Hearn 2013a). In other respects, dependency theory has ingrained Brazilian distrust of foreign superpowers, including China, which stands accused of neocolonial ambitions and inadequate transparency (Maciel and Nedal 2011; *Estadão* 2010).

Elements of dependency theory continue to influence Brazilian public debate. As Selene Martínez Pacheco writes, "One of the common claims amongst the group that opposes Chinese influence in Brazil is that China is treating Brazil as a colony, taking Brazil's development backwards" (2014: 118). FIESP is among several prominent institutions that perceives a deepening risk of overreliance on commodities, which between iron ore, oil, and soy constitute 80 percent of Brazil's exports to China (Fellet 2011; Landim 2012a, 2012b; Schneider 2012). The economy, say the critics, is overexposed not only to the volatility of commodity prices, but also to deindustrialization as the resource sector drives up the exchange rate and undermines the competitiveness of national manufacturers. The impact of this "Dutch Disease" is allegedly intensified by Chinese currency manipulation, which artificially suppresses the price of Chinese manufactured exports, putting Brazilian manufacturers out of business as cheap alternatives inundate the market.

Conscious of these critiques, Chinese researchers contend that their nation is empathetic toward Latin America's colonial past and sensitive to the need for poverty alleviation. Jiang Shixue, for instance, argues that China's relations with the region should be understood not as neocolonialism but as South-South cooperation, because China, unlike colonial predecessors, has inflated rather than depressed commodity prices and reduced rather than increased the price of manufactured goods. Furthermore, he writes, "while colonial powers sought to monopolize markets by discouraging the development of industries in their colonies, China invests actively in technology transfer programs, which have assisted the development of local industries across the continent" (2011: 62–63).

To demonstrate its disposition to invest in locally beneficial initiatives, in 2010 Chongqing Grain Corporation signed an agreement with the government of Bahia state to build a soybean processing complex near the town of Barreiras. The proposed $300 million investment was to be the first of six facilities (totaling $2 billion) that would crush soybeans to produce soymeal and soy oil, adding value in Brazil rather than in China. The plant would employ local workers, source soybeans from the immediate region around Barreiras, and reserve a proportion of the soy oil and meal it produced for the local market. By promising local benefit and added value, the project distinguished itself from previous colonial endeavors and attempted to alleviate concerns about the negative implications of Chinese investment.

As an incentive for the investment, the mayor of Barreiras provided Chongqing with 100 hectares for the plant to stand on, adding to the firm's existing bid for 100,000 hectares of farmland (CBBC 2011: 26; Powell 2011). But the powerful Landless Rural Workers' Movement (MST) criticized the scale of the acquisition, joining a coalition of civil and environmental advocates to describe it as a land grab. Chongqing's status as a Chinese government enterprise deepened suspicions of its motives, as articulated by CBBC chairman Sergio Amaral: "Sometimes you don't know whether the investments are looking for Brazil as a market or whether they correspond to strategic purposes of the Chinese government" (quoted in Pyne 2010). Or in the words of the newspaper *Estadão* (2010), Chinese financiers "may act according to commercial interests, like other investors, but may follow the logic of a state—and not the Brazilian state."

These doubts, accompanied by the new federal limits on foreign landownership, have bemused Chinese officials such as Zhang Dongxiang, chief executive officer of the Bank of China's Brazil branch: "Public opinion sometimes seems to be against foreign investment . . . as if it makes local industry less competitive. . . . [T]hese are some antiquated ideas" (quoted in Winter and Stauffer 2013). The Barreiras project was effectively shelved, having received approximately 15 percent of the projected $2 billion by late 2014, and most of this in assessment and mapping activities.

Chinese president Xi Jinping visited Brazil amid these tensions in July 2014 to sign an $8.6 billion investment agreement including a railway to transport soybeans and iron ore to Peru's Pacific coast. Charles Tang, chairman of the Brazil-China Chamber of Commerce, described the project as mutually beneficial: "China has a strong interest in Brazilian commodities, so they want to invest in railroads in Brazil to reduce transport costs. This is a win-win situation, because the Brazilian government wants to attract investments in infrastructure" (quoted in Trevisani and Jelmayer 2014). Pragmatism notwithstanding, clarifying and publicly communicating the motives driving Chinese SOE investments is becoming increasingly important for the Brazilian government and its counterparts in other resource-exporting nations.

Brazil's experience of Chinese investment underscores the difficulty of attracting finance into locally beneficial agriculture projects. Resource-seeking finance has done little to add value, transfer technology, upgrade infrastructure, or teach new skills to employees. The Barreiras soy-processing initiative and President Xi's 2014 rail proposal imply more mutually agreeable outcomes, but have yet to materialize. Australia faces similar challenges as Chinese investment increasingly targets the agriculture sector.

Legalizing Dissent in Australia

In April 2014, Australian prime minister Tony Abbott told a business convention in Shanghai that "we now appreciate that most Chinese state-owned enterprises have a highly commercial culture. . . . They're not the nationalised industries that we used to have in Australia" (quoted in Kenny and Wen 2014). The statement departed from his speech in Beijing two years earlier while leader of the opposition Liberal National Party: "It would rarely be in Australia's interests to allow a foreign government or its agencies to control an Australian business. . . . That's because we don't support the nationalisation of businesses by the Australian government, let alone a foreign one. . . . The next Coalition government will stand up for Australia's interests and values" (quoted in Garnaut 2012).

Ambivalent statements about Chinese investment reveal uncertainty about what—if any—national interests this investment could threaten and how the risks stack up against the benefits. The TPP could furnish the Australian and other member governments with an instrument for managing this politically sensitive terrain. Citing TPP restrictions on SOEs would allow them to demonstrate to voters their vigilance against unwelcome advances by foreign states, while a range of loopholes and exceptions would enable them to continue courting Chinese finance. As a multilateral endeavor, the TPP also enables ambiguity overseas: governments could use it to voice concerns about Chinese government finance without singling themselves out as anti-Chinese and risking repercussions from Beijing.

Australians are accustomed to large Chinese investments in the mining sector, which amounted to US$37 billion between 2006 and 2012 (Ferguson and Hendrischke 2013: 6). Total Chinese investments in Australia in that period reached $51 billion, more than any other country, and rose to $60 billion in 2014. As Saul Eslake has written, Australia is "unusual for an advanced economy" in its reliance on Asian natural resource markets, and in that only 16 percent of its exports are manufactured goods (2011: 145). The recent surge of interest from Chinese agriculture investors therefore fits an established pattern, though one that did not previously evoke such impassioned reactions.

In November 2012, the Shanghai Zhongfu Group proposed to invest US$730 million (AU$700 million) to lease 15,000 hectares of arable land in North West Australia's Ord Valley for fifty years, with a view to exporting sugar to China for production of biofuels. Since the land was to be rented rather than bought, the investment went ahead without the need for assessment by Australia's Foreign Investment Review Board (FIRB). Having secured the land, Shanghai Zhongfu noted that the unexpectedly harsh weather was more appropriate for the production of grains and indicated its interest in leasing a further 15,000 hectares. Opponents criticized the downward impact the deal could have on crop prices as Ord production ramps up, the possible influx of Chinese workers, environmental and taxation concessions granted to the Chinese firm, and the prospect that "China is set to swoop on one of northern Australia's most important—and biggest—land and water resources" (White 2012; also see Murray and Grigg 2013). Although Shanghai Zhongfu is a private company, the China Development Bank has offered to support it, and according to one report "it is unclear whether Shanghai Zhongfu, which trades in Australia as Kimberley Agricultural Investments, is owned by the Chinese Government" (White 2012).

Similar concerns emerged when Shandong Ruyi Woolen Textile Company spent US$277 million (AU$265 million) to acquire 80 percent of Cubbie Station, a 93,000-hectare cotton plantation in the state of Queensland and the Southern Hemisphere's largest irrigated property. Public complaints about Chinese government influence led Treasurer Wayne Swan to require Shandong Ruyi to sell down its shares in Cubbie Station to 51 percent within three years, but opponents argued that Chinese state enterprises would likely acquire the available shares through private subsidiaries. Furthermore, Liberal Party senator Bill Heffernan warned that Shandong Ruyi may pursue political rather than economic goals, selling cotton to its government at suppressed prices in order to minimize taxable income: "If someone produces something but it's not for sale, how do you tax it?" (quoted in Crowe 2012). This practice, known as price transfer, remains a key common concern in Australia and Brazil.

In response to the publicity generated by these cases, in 2012 the Liberal National Party (elected to government in 2013) released a policy paper on foreign investment in Australian agricultural land and agribusiness. The paper endorses existing legislation that requires the FIRB to assess the national benefit of any land acquisition proposed by a foreign SOE and that requires "other classes" of investment (i.e., private) to trigger FIRB scrutiny at 15 percent or more of a business valued upward of AU$244 million. The paper also signals that "the creeping cumulative acquisition of agricultural land . . . may be inconsistent with both the national interest and the interests of local communities" and that a coalition working group had been established "to investigate options to strengthen the rules governing the sale of agricultural land and agribusinesses to foreign entities" (Liberal National Party of Australia 2012: 3–4).

Headed by National Party leader Warren Truss, who in mid-2013 warned that "we have lost control of our nation's agribusinesses," the working group has argued that any investment over the value of US$13.5 million (AU$15 million) should be subjected to FIRB scrutiny (Liberal National Party of Australia 2012: 12). Pressed on the issue after winning office in 2013, Joe Hockey, treasurer of the coalition working group, indicated that Chinese firms could be exempted from this scrutiny under the Australia-China FTA. The two governments signed off on the FTA in late 2014, shortly after announcing that the Chinese SOE Beijing Agricultural Investment Fund would invest $3 billion in Australian dairy, beef, lamb, and aquaculture assets.

The coalition paper proposes that foreign investors be required to disclose "any direct or indirect ownership or direct source of influence by a foreign government, such as a state-owned enterprise owning shares in a subsidiary related to the business operation of the applicant" (Liberal National Party of Australia 2012: 14). But beyond this it does not specify the criteria by which enterprises are deemed to be state-owned. Previous determinations have deferred to the legal status of the enterprise in its home country, but like the coalition paper they have not sought to discern the extent to which ostensibly private investors benefit from indirect state support. This support might include preferential access to finance, fast-track approvals, discounted logistical services, commitments to buying their exports for fixed timeframes, and other incentives to offset below-market pricing of their output.

Blanket restrictions on SOEs, as proposed by some TPP enthusiasts, will not resolve the risks associated with SOE investment. Limits on the shareholding stakes that SOEs can pursue in companies listed in TPP countries, requirements that they source inputs (including employees) from private rather than public sector providers, and obligations to report subsidies, discounts, and pricing commitments all look good on paper. In theory, rules such as these should establish a legal framework for managing an increasingly sensitive issue that until now has been regulated in response to informal pressure from opinion pages and outspoken politicians. For all their precision, though, these measures will not prevent Chinese and other SOEs from working with business partners in recipient nations to develop countermeasures and exploit loopholes.

SOE Countermeasures

The TPP would elicit responses from Chinese SOEs that have previously served their interests in the face of regulatory barriers. For instance, following the rejection of Chinese mining SOE Chinalco's bid to become the dominant shareholder in Australian mining giant Rio Tinto in 2009, Chinese investors targeted smaller, cumulative stakes in Australian firms (Larum 2013). The TPP would pressure foreign SOEs to pursue less "vertical" investment practices, but past experience suggests that it would also motivate them to explore legal loopholes and exceptions.

Despite pressure from activist groups, the TPP negotiations did not clearly determine whether state-level SOEs should be treated the same way as national-level SOEs, leaving open the possibility of state-level subsidiaries acting on behalf of their national parent enterprises. Debate on this issue in Australia has focused on implications for the health sector, which could face diminished support for state-level public hospitals, but the level at which SOEs are defined will also bear relevance to mining, agriculture, and other sectors receiving inbound investment from Chinese government sources. In contrast to the TPP's ostensibly high-quality "gold standard" commitments, domestic actors across most member countries wish to see state-level SOEs exempted from "competitive neutrality" requirements. Fortunately for these actors, political differences between TPP governments favor a broad, national-level interpretation. For Chinese SOEs looking to invest in TPP countries, this will encourage delegation to state-level subsidiaries to manage the negotiation and daily operation of projects.[4] As the Organization for Economic Cooperation and Development rightly observes, "political considerations sometimes play a direct role in the categorisation of SOEs" (OECD 2012: 33).

Chinese SOEs are also likely to respond to the TPP by channeling investments through private firms in which they hold shares or exercise influence. From 2006 to 2012, at least 35 percent (by value) of Chinese agricultural investments in Australia were private (the total from all Chinese sources for that period was $1.05 billion) (Ferguson and Hendrischke 2013: 13).[5] Private firms that invest in Australia are not subjected to the FIRB's national interest test unless they purchase 15 percent or more of a business worth US$190 million (AU$244 million). Public anxiety over inbound Chinese investment is not limited to SOEs, as the Shanghai Zhongfu–Ord Valley deal showed. Indeed, critics argued that although Shanghai Zhongfu is a private enterprise, it has benefited from obscure, market-distorting approvals and funding concessions in China. Nevertheless, characterizing investments as private rather than state-owned may diminish public opposition in recipient countries and, critically, circumvent the TPP's proposed restrictions on SOEs.[6]

A related method for injecting public finance into the private sector is the acquisition of established private actors. China's largest agriculture SOE, the China National Cereals, Oils, and Foodstuffs Corporation (COFCO), demonstrated this strategy in 2014, paying $1.2 billion for 51 percent of Dutch grain trader Nidera and $1.5 billion for 51 percent of Singapore-based Noble

Group. COFCO's acquisition of both companies' assets in Australia and Brazil enable it to diminish China's reliance on the Big Four multinational grain suppliers. By leaving Noble and Nidera's executive boards, administrative structures, and employment practices largely unchanged, COFCO has diminished perceptions of Chinese government aggression.

COFCO previously pursued a similar approach in Australia, where its $136 million acquisition of Tully Sugar in 2011 provoked concerns about "selling off the farm" and replacing the local work force with less expensive Chinese labor (Fraser and Elks 2011). In response to these worries, COFCO recruited an Australian chief executive officer and executive team at Tully, and its vice president, Li Ming, promised "to create jobs, not to take them" (Ferguson, Hendrischke, and Barber 2014: 40). It also donated resources to local schools and community clubs and made assurances that Tully's produce would sell on the open market, making it "just as likely to end up in Europe as China" (quoted in Neales 2012). These measures have largely mitigated local perceptions of Chinese state expansionism, and if undertaken by a private enterprise such as Noble or Nidera would also sidestep TPP restrictions on SOEs.

The Chinese government has already begun to offset the TPP's potential impact by forging bilateral FTAs that would take precedence over TPP rules. This process is under way in the China-Australia FTA, with the added purpose of appeasing Beijing's discomfort with the US-Australia-Japan strategic alliance (Song and Yuan 2012: 112–113; Yang 2008). By early 2015 China had concluded eleven bilateral FTAs, one with the Association of Southeast Asian Nations (ASEAN), and was negotiating a further two. A priority for Australian negotiators has been to reduce China's 21 percent import tariff on agriculture products, but Chinese negotiators have insisted that in return they want the FIRB scrutiny threshold (for state and private finance) increased to match that applied to investments into Australia from the United States and New Zealand. Having concluded FTAs with the United States and New Zealand in 2009 and 1983, Australia requires no FIRB scrutiny of deals valued under AU$1 billion (US$780 million).

These countermeasures will enable the Chinese government to continue investing in TPP countries and advancing its vision of regional integration. TPP nations must consider the implications of acquiescence to this vision, and to do so effectively will require case-by-case assessments of investment proposals from both state and private sources.

Conclusion

As the Chinese government plots a course through unprecedented development challenges, concerns over food security loom large. Driven first and foremost by domestic pressures, China's leaders have identified greater agricultural self-sufficiency as a strategic priority. To this end, the NDRC has rolled out a nationwide program of technical upgrading, irrigation efficiency, and transgenic grain production. The results of these initiatives will become evident over the coming decade, a critical period for China's development as the urban population edges toward the target of 860 million by 2020. In the meantime, China will continue to import massive quantities of grains, meat, dairy, and other foods and to seek opportunities for outbound agriculture investments.

The Brazilian and Australian cases reveal sensitivity about Chinese inbound investment in agriculture, a sector that evokes emotional connections to land, occupation, and food. As Chinese finance increasingly targets foreign food production, public concerns about territorial sovereignty are likely to become stronger and louder. Managing public reactions to Chinese investment is a growing challenge for the Brazilian and Australian governments, which have each introduced stricter regulations on inbound capital in the agriculture sector. A functioning TPP would mark a divergence in the two nations' circumstances, as it would affect how Australian regulators assess investment proposals.

Brazil's turbulent experience of Chinese investment has evolved from general enthusiasm during Hu Jintao's 2004 landmark Latin America tour to a more recent critical debate about resource-seeking versus value-adding finance. President Xi Jinping's visit a decade later emphasized China's disposition to invest in rail and infrastructure, but Brazilians are deferring celebrations until they see results. Cynicism will endure unless resulting projects stimulate activity beyond the export of raw soybeans. Chongqing Grain Corporation's proposed soy-processing plant in Barreiras affords hope that Chinese finance can add value, but its characterization as a land grab, coupled with federal limits on foreign land acquisition, has impeded the project's completion. The case demonstrates a growing need for more sophisticated mechanisms for formally evaluating and communicating the risks and benefits posed by specific investments.

Like their Brazilian counterparts, Australians are wary of Chinese agriculture investment and have struggled to formulate an effective framework for assessing national benefit. The TPP could help in this regard, but its chapter on investment, alongside the recommendations of conservative think tanks, is encumbered by a preoccupation with curtailing public finance. Provisions to identify and limit the activities of SOEs may promote a broader mix of public and private activity in some sectors, but they offer a blunt solution to a complex problem. A more sophisticated approach would encourage governments to assess investment proposals on a case-by-case basis for their merits and detriments. These include their potential to conform to environmental regulations, generate local employment, and add value to national industries; and to disrupt or displace domestic production, avoid taxation through profit shifting and price transfer, and monopolize chains of production and logistics. Such assessments should apply equally to public and private investments, which both have mixed track records on these criteria.

The European Union's approach to evaluating threats and opportunities arising from foreign investment is instructive, as its vigilance toward SOEs arises not from government ownership per se but from the likelihood of anticompetitive behavior. As former European commissioner for competition policy Joaquín Almunia (2011) explains: "We look carefully at whether, through the State, companies in the same sector act as one or different entities. This is not because they are foreign or we have a prejudice against State control, but because it is a relevant aspect for assessing if competition will be significantly reduced or not."

Assessing proposals on a case-by-case basis for competitive impact, capacity to add value, generate employment, and the like avoids the risks of ascribing behavioral expectations to public (and private) enterprises. Among the risks of a one-size-fits-all approach to SOEs is the proliferation of countermeasures to circumvent restrictions. Some countermeasures may be lawful, such as the pursuit of FTAs that carve out exemptions to—and ultimately dilute the influence of—the TPP. More underhanded variants include surreptitious delegation from federal to less restricted state-level SOE subsidiaries, channeling of public finance through colluding private firms, and price transfer to avoid taxation.

Recent Australian and Brazilian experiences demonstrate the domestic political fallout that can result from Chinese investment, but also the resulting opportunities to climb food and agriculture value chains through processing and infrastructure development. In light of Premier Li Keqiang's plan to invest $500 billion overseas by 2018, TPP nations should formulate strategies that contain the risks and harness the benefits of China's international expansion. Commitments to limiting the activities of SOEs under the TPP should therefore be accompanied by efforts to understand the range of formal and informal countermeasures that Chinese investors have begun to employ. How Asia Pacific nations balance these commitments and countermeasures will condition the evolution of regional integration.

Notes

1. Monetary values are in US dollars unless otherwise indicated, in which case backdated exchange rates are used.

2. These firms, known informally as the Big Four, or the ABCD, have each faced obstacles in the growth of their Australian operations, the latest resulting from the 2013 bid of Archer Daniels Midlands to acquire Australia's Graincorp for

US$3.2 billion. Deputy Prime Minister Warren Truss opposed the acquisition, arguing that "if we lose this business to foreign ownership, then we will lose the potential to have an international standard agribusiness trading around the world." Shortly after, in November the same year, Treasurer Joe Hockey announced that the investment would be contrary to national interests and prohibited it. See Kelly and Maher 2013.

3. Similarly in Argentina, opponents of a bid by Chinese firm Heilongjian Beidahuang Nongken Group to rent 320,000 hectares to grow soybeans in Río Negro province used social media to describe the project as a "neocolonial land grab" and successfully pressured the Argentine congress to cancel the contract. Foreign landownership was subsequently limited to 1,000 hectares, not to exceed 15 percent of any property.

4. Another loophole concerns employment. The TPP would limit the ability of SOEs to recruit and arrange visas en masse for agricultural and other workers. However, it would not inhibit employers from classifying these individuals as independent technicians or even as tourists.

5. According to Doug Ferguson and Hans Hendrischke, the proportion of Chinese public and private ownership of Australian assets cannot be precisely determined because smaller holdings are not registered: "Until we have a national record of foreign ownership of Australian land that looks through the corporate veil, it will be difficult to establish the extent of Chinese ownership below USD 5 million" (2013: 7).

6. Leasing rather than buying land is another strategy that Chinese firms, including Shanghai Zhongfu, have employed to bypass regulatory restrictions. It is not yet clear if the TPP could be leveraged to close this loophole.

10

Harnessing the Currents of Asia Pacific Integration

Adrian H. Hearn and Margaret Myers

TWO CURRENTS ARE SHAPING THE DYNAMICS OF ASIA PACIFIC ECO-nomic integration in the twenty-first century. One of these is China's emergence as a superpower, a process that became progressively evident as financial crises in the 1990s and 2000s shook global markets and intensified Chinese outward economic and political engagement. The other is a renewed push under the US-led Trans-Pacific Partnership (TPP) to redefine the parameters of multilateral cooperation. The prior current enabled the injection of over $20 billion of Chinese foreign direct investment (FDI) into Association of Southeast Asian Nations members between 2012 and 2014, consolidating the bloc's regional preeminence (ASEAN 2015). The latter current aspires to push the frontiers of liberalization "behind the borders" of TPP members to govern financial flows, state-owned enterprises (SOEs), intellectual property, investor-state disputes, and other matters previously beyond the remit of multilateral agreements. In a region where government social services, subsidized health programs, protected sectors, and top-down industrial policies are the norm, the two currents are naturally generating turbulence.

Faced simultaneously with China's rise and the TPP's liberalization agenda, Asia Pacific nations are seeking to balance the opportunities and risks. Domestic market reforms are part of their response, but so are defensive strategies to conserve the existing order. To provide a flexible multilateral framework that might strike this balance, the ten ASEAN nations and their six free trade agreement (FTA) partners are formulating the Regional Comprehensive Economic Partnership (RCEP). The initiative aims to liberalize trade and investment, but its lenience on how and when members reduce tariffs, define rules of origin, and implement reforms provides sufficient leeway to forestall change. Officially led by ASEAN, China is the driving force behind this regional counterpoint to the TPP.

The distinct visions of regional order proposed by RCEP and the TPP are among several countercurrents simmering below the surface of

US-China relations. Another is the China-led Asian Infrastructure Investment Bank (AIIB), which is widely seen as a direct challenge to the US-dominated Bretton Woods system of monetary management. As former US treasury secretary Larry Summers has stated, "We're contemplating a major institution in which the United States has no role" (quoted in Zarroli 2015). The United States initially opposed the AIIB's formation, citing concerns that the bank would issue finance with little regard for international standards of governance and transparency. These concerns derive from the lending records of China's major policy banks (China Development Bank and China Eximbank), which have focused heavily on overseas extractive and infrastructure sectors while attaching few policy conditions to their loans. Fifty-seven countries have signed on as charter members of the AIIB, including some of the closest allies of the United States, effectively silencing US critics.

How these distinct initiatives coincide and diverge will become clearer over the long term, but in the interim other countercurrents threaten to boil over. The most pressing of these are territorial disputes in the South China Sea, which cannot be quarantined from trade and investment negotiations. RCEP and the TPP are inextricable from strategic affairs because China's maritime claims are contested by Japan, the Philippines, and other RCEP members, while US military ties are embraced by Australia, Vietnam, and other TPP members. As Jianmin Jin notes in Chapter 3 of this volume, the statements of US officials and commentators that the TPP is linked to security concerns weighs heavily on Chinese minds.

With $590 billion of bilateral trade in 2014, the US and Chinese economies are deeply intertwined, providing a strong disincentive for conflict (US Census Bureau 2015). Their interpenetration will deepen if the US-China bilateral investment treaty (BIT), under negotiation since 2008 and prioritized since 2014, boosts two-way investment as expected. In 2012, US finance represented only about 1.2 percent of China's total inward FDI, while China accounts for an even smaller share of FDI into the United States (Bergsten et al. 2015). Key to the agreement is China's commitment to protect US investments at all stages of development and in all sectors not explicitly ruled out by a negative list. China stands to benefit by boosting domestic economic growth through inbound finance into a range of productive sectors and through outbound finance into US infrastructure, power generation, and information technology. The United States stands to benefit from the agreement's removal of restrictions on capital flows into and out of China, its nullification of performance rules requiring local content in manufactured products, its guarantee against discrimination and expropriation of US assets, and the access it opens to China's nascent services sector.

The US-China BIT confirms this volume's finding that the two nations' interests are not inimical to each other, and in many respects they overlap. Closer integration with the United States is fundamental to the Chinese government's attempt to fashion an urban, middle-income nation whose growth is led by domestic consumption of global products and services. This goal is paramount to Chinese leaders as it provides the best chance for social stability and, hence, political longevity. Conversely, closer integration with China enables the United States to advance a "behind the border" liberalization agenda that many in Washington envision as a blueprint for global reform. Whether or not this blueprint is eventually adopted, the prospects for Sino-US symbiosis are strong, substantiating President Barack Obama's June 2015 remark that China is "putting out feelers" to assess potential TPP membership.

The Xi Jinping administration's steps to boost consumption, liberalize services, and negotiate tariff reductions have been slowed by domestic interest groups spanning from automobile producers to its own ministries. The scandals gripping the State-Owned Assets Supervision and Administration Commission (SASAC), which is responsible for reforming the nation's SOEs, and the government's controversial anticorruption campaign demonstrate the fraught nature of political change. The TPP coincides with several aspects of the Chinese government's reform agenda, and it has therefore attracted conciliatory appraisals from Premier Li Keqiang, Commerce Ministry official Sun Yuanjiang, and others. For China's reformers, the TPP could serve a similar purpose to that of the World Trade Organization (WTO), which has provided a global mechanism for domestic growth. This local-global connection was articulated by Vice Finance Minister Zhu Guangyao in 2014: "As China becomes more open, it's very important for us to be integrated into the global trade system with a high standard" (quoted in Bradsher 2015).

Under negotiation since 2005, the TPP's long journey to ratification was energized in mid-2015 when the US House of Representatives awarded President Obama trade promotion authority. This enabled him to directly negotiate the TPP on behalf of the United States and fast-track executive decisions through Congress. Denial of trade promotion authority would have derailed the TPP after more than twenty rounds of painstaking negotiation because Japan, Canada, and other participating countries were unwilling to pledge reforms unless the US Congress was prevented from subsequently amending the deal. Trade promotion authority guaranteed this and vindicated the TPP as the centerpiece of US economic policy in the Asia Pacific.

The conclusion of TPP negotiations in October 2015 and signing ceremony in February 2016 brought the agreement one step closer to implementation. However, as Canadian trade minister Chrystia Freeland has stated, "Signing does not equal ratifying. . . . Signing is simply a technical step in the process, allowing the TPP text to be tabled in Parliament for consideration and debate before any final decision is made" (quoted in Blatchford 2016). As the twelve member governments conduct national debates to determine whether or not to ratify the TPP, several pressing concerns guide their deliberations. Among these are apprehensions about the TPP's provisions for (1) extending corporate intellectual property rights, (2) permitting foreign investors to use international arbitration to challenge sovereign governments that introduce commercially unfavorable laws, and (3) reducing the economic capacities of state-owned enterprises.

To be implemented, the TPP must be ratified by at least six signatories, whose combined gross domestic product (GDP) must amount to at least 85 percent of the collective total. The deal will therefore only progress if ratified by the United States and Japan, whose combined GDP amounts to more than two-thirds of the total. US ratification is uncertain because all leading contenders in the US presidential race oppose the TPP. A characteristically garish statement from Donald Trump suggested the agreement's openness to abuse by China: "The TPP is a horrible deal. . . . It is a deal that is going to lead to nothing but trouble. It's a deal that was designed for China to come in, as they always do, through the back door and totally take advantage of everyone" (quoted in Brinkley 2016). The statement does not square with estimates that the TPP is likely to divert $100 billion of trade away from China in the first decade and redirect investment in low-wage industries from China to Vietnam (Gary Hufbauer, cited in Weissmann 2015). Analyses of China's relationship with the TPP vary in sobriety, but this volume shows that the TPP does raise uncertainties and questions for future research as the Asia Pacific region becomes increasingly reliant on Chinese trade and investment:

- Can the TPP enable members to diversify their exports in high-value-added sectors without compromising their existing exports to (and imports from) China?
- To what extent does China's expanding network of bilateral FTAs, and efforts to articulate them with RCEP, work against or overlap with the TPP?
- Would more flexible, country-specific terms for the future induction of additional nations into the TPP strengthen the prospect of eventual Chinese membership?
- How will the TPP's proposed restrictions on state-owned enterprises impact recent efforts in Chile, Peru, Australia, and other signatories to attract foreign investment into agriculture and infrastructure from Chinese (and other) government sources?

- To what extent can the proposed Free Trade Area of the Asia Pacific (FTAAP) accommodate the distinct visions of integration proposed by the TPP and RCEP, and thereby avoid deepening rivalry between China and the United States?

As US and Chinese visions of economic governance refashion the architecture of global trade and investment, some Asia Pacific regions will emerge as testing grounds for their interaction. Latin America is a likely forerunner, having received more than $130 billion in loans from China since 2005—more than the combined loans of the World Bank, the Inter-American Development Bank, and the US Export Import Bank. TPP members Chile and Peru have leveraged maximum benefit from this evolving scenario by establishing parallel agreements with the United States and China. Both nations' FTAs with the United States, signed in 2004 and 2009, respectively, feature provisions that resemble the TPP's "twenty-first-century" standards. Their FTAs with China, signed in 2005 and 2009, contain conditions for market access and rules of origin similar to RCEP's. China has also signed bilateral investment agreements with Colombia, Mexico, and Peru, whose arbitration chapters appear to be modeled on prior US frameworks, providing an exploratory bridge between Chinese and US approaches (Irwin 2014).

As they seek to harness the changing currents of transpacific integration, the United States and China will become intertwined in increasingly overlapping interests. These include trade, investment, connectivity, and security, and they will generate both competitive tensions and cooperative opportunities. The TPP and RCEP approach these collective interests with differing scope, depth, and flexibility and therefore invite hasty zero-sum assessments. The two initiatives nevertheless harbor sufficient complementarity to interact less as countercurrents than as a shared tidal force for change. The TPP's insistence on market efficiency and RCEP's responsiveness to social concerns could together constitute a comprehensive and balanced framework. They offer the clearest pathway to untangling the "noodle bowl" of existing bilateral FTAs and replacing it with harmonized mega-regional alternatives. Overlapping commitments are emblematic of twenty-first-century economic diplomacy, begging the question to what extent the TPP, RCEP, and their advocates will themselves find mutual balance.

Bibliography

Adams, Christopher (2012) "Crafar dairy farms deal finally settled." *New Zealand Herald,* 1 December.

Almunia, Joaquín (2011) "Recent developments and future priorities in EU competition policy." Speech to the International Competition Law Forum, St. Gallen, 8 April.

Amnesty International (2012) "TPP must not trade away free speech and health." Amnesty International Media Centre. www.amnesty.org/en/for-media/press-releases/tpp-must-not-trade-away-free-speech-and-health-2012-09-06.

Anderson, Sarah (2011) *Capital Controls and the Trans-Pacific Partnership.* Washington, DC: Institute for Policy Studies.

APEC (Asia Pacific Economic Cooperation forum) (2014) "2014 meeting of APEC ministers responsible for trade." *APEC Ministerial Statements,* 17–18 May. http://apec.org/Meeting-Papers/Ministerial-Statements/Trade/2014_trade.aspx.

ASEAN (Association of Southeast Asian Nations) (2013) "Regional Comprehensive Economic Partnership (RCEP): Joint statement the first meeting of trade negotiating committee." www.asean.org.

——— (2015) "Table 26: Foreign direct investment net inflows in ASEAN from selected partner countries/regions." *ASEAN Foreign Direct Investment Statistics Database.* www.asean.org/news/item/foreign-direct-investment-statistics.

Barboza, David (2008) "Chinese destroy 3,600 tons of tainted feed: Officials destroy tons of melamine-laced feed for livestock." *New York Times,* 3 November.

Barfield, Claude (2011) "The Trans-Pacific Partnership: A model for twenty-first-century trade agreements?" International Economic Outlook series, no. 2 (June). Washington, DC: American Enterprise Institute, pp. 1–8.

Basu Das, Sanchita (2013a) "RCEP and TPP: Comparisons and concerns." *ISEAS Perspective* (January). www.iseas.edu.sg/documents/publication/ISEAS%20Perspective%202013_2.pdf.

——— (2013b) "The Trans-Pacific Partnership as a tool to contain China: Myth or reality?" *East Asia Forum,* 8 June. www.eastasiaforum.org.

Baughn, C. Christopher, and Attila Yaprak (1996) "Economic nationalism: Conceptual and empirical development." *Political Psychology* 17, pp. 759–778.

BBC (British Broadcasting Corporation) (2015) "China cautiously welcomes Trans-Pacific free trade deal." *BBC News,* 6 October. www.bbc.com.

Beeson, Mark (2007) *Globalization, Regionalism, and Nationalism in East Asia.* London: Palgrave Macmillan.

Beeson, Mark, and Fujian Li (2012) "Charmed or alarmed? Reading China's regional relations." *Journal of Contemporary China* 21, no. 73, pp. 35–51.

——— (2014) *China's Regional Relations: Evolving Foreign Policy Dynamics.* Boulder: Lynne Rienner.

Bergsten, C. Fred (2006) *The Free Trade Area of the Asia Pacific Is the Next Step Forward for APEC (and for the World Trading System).* Washington, DC: Peterson Institute for International Economics, November.

——— (2015) "Currency manipulation: Why something must be done." *Forbes,* 25 February. www.forbes.com.

Bergsten, C. Fred, et al. (2015) "Toward a U.S.-China investment treaty." Brief no. 15-1. Washington, DC: Peterson Institute of International Economics, February. www.iie.com/publications/interstitial.cfm?ResearchID=2748.

Bi, Mingxin (2013) "S. Korea, China narrow differences in 6th FTA talks." *Xinhua,* 4 July. http://news.xinhuanet.com.

Birdsall, Nancy (2002) "Asymmetric globalization: Global markets require good global politics." Washington, DC: Center for Global Development. www.rrojasdatabank.info/widerconf/Birdsall.pdf.

Bisley, Nick (2012) "China's rise and the making of East Asia's security architecture." *Journal of Contemporary China* 21, no. 73, pp. 19–34.

Blatchford, Andy (2016) "Canada will sign TPP trade deal Feb. 4, but ratification not certain." *CBC News,* 25 January. www.cbc.ca.

Boris, Joseph (2013) "China studies giant Pacific trade pact." *China Daily,* 31 June. http://usa.chinadaily.com.cn.

Bowles, Paul (2014) "China debates the TPP." *East Asia Forum,* 20 March. www.eastasiaforum.org.

Bradsher, Keith (2015) "Once concerned, China is quiet about trans-pacific trade deal." *New York Times,* 28 April.

Brinkley, John (2016) "Donald Trump: Stalking the wild TPP." *Forbes,* 12 November. www.forbes.com.

Busch, Lawrence (2004) "Grades and standards in the social construction of safe food." In *The Politics of Food,* edited by M. E. Lien, pp. 163–178. Oxford: Berg.

Cai, Penghong (2011) "The Trans-Pacific Partnership: A Chinese perspective." Presentation delivered at the 20th PECC General Meeting, Washington, DC. www.pecc.org/resources/cat_view/44-trade-and-investment?limit=40&order=name&dir=DESC.

Caixin Online (2013) "Closer look: How agreements like the TPP press China to reform." 30 October. http://english.caixin.com.

Campbell, Kurt, and Brian Andrews (2013) *Explaining the US "Pivot" to Asia.* Chatham House Programme Paper Series. https://www.chathamhouse.org/sites/files/chathamhouse/public/Research/Americas/0813pp_pivottoasia.pdf.

Capaldo, Jeronim, Alex Izurieta, and Jomo Kwame Sundaram (2016) "Trading down: Unemployment, inequality, and other risks of the Trans-Pacific Partnership agreement." Working Paper no. 16-01. Medford, MA: Global Development and Environment Institute, January.

Cardoso, Fernando (2001) *Charting a New Course: The Politics of Globalization and Social Transformation.* Lanham: Rowman and Littlefield.

Cardoso, Fernando, and Enzo Faletto (1979) *Dependency and Development in Latin America.* Berkeley: University of California Press.

Carter, Ashton (2015) "Remarks on the next phase of the U.S. rebalance to the Asia-Pacific." Washington, DC: US Department of Defense, 6 April. www.defense.gov/Speeches/Speech.aspx?SpeechID=1929.

CBBC (China-Brazil Business Council) (2011) *Chinese Investments in Brazil: A New Phase in the China-Brazil Relationship*. Rio.

Celikkol, Ömer Orhun (2013) "The implications of new age FTAs in the Asia-Pacific: TPP and RCEP." *International Covenant on Economic Issues*, May. www.mfa.gov.tr/site_media/html/ekonomiksorunlardergisi/sayi46.pdf#page=60.

Cha, Victor (2009) "Powerplay: Origins of the US alliance system in Asia." *International Security* 34, no. 3, pp. 158–196.

Chang, Gordon (2015) "TPP vs. RCEP: America and China battle for control of Pacific trade." *National Interest*, 6 October. http://nationalinterest.org.

Chen, Dongxiao (2015) "China aims to set the regional cooperation agenda." *East Asia Forum*, 28 July. www.eastasiaforum.org.

China Daily (2004) "Hu hails friendship with all Latin America." 14 November. www.chinadaily.com.

——— (2013) "China hopes for transparent US-led TPP talks." 31 May. http://usa.chinadaily.com.

Chinese Ministry of Foreign Affairs (2013) "Waijiaobu Jiu Xi Jinping Zhuxi Fangwen Yindunixiya, Malaixiya, Bing Chuxi Yatai Jinghe Zuzhi Di Ershiyi Ci Lingdaoren Feizhengshi Huiyi Juxing Zhongwai Meiti Chuifenghui" (MFA media briefing on President Xi Jinping's visit to Indonesia and Malaysia and attendance at the twenty-first informal summit of APEC leaders). 29 September. www.gov.cn/gzdt/2013-09/30/content_2498101.htm.

Chosun Media (2013) "Korea to join Trans-Pacific Partnership." 9 September. http://english.chosun.com.

Chung, Chien-peng (2008) "China's approaches to the institutionalization of regional multilateralism." *Journal of Contemporary China* 17, no. 57, pp. 747–764.

Clement, Wallace (1983) "Uneven development: A mature branch plant society." In *Class, Power, and Property: Essays on Canadian Society*, edited by W. Clement, pp. 55–84. Toronto: Methuen.

Coelho, Bruno, and Kevin P. Gallagher (2013) "The effectiveness of capital controls: Evidence from Colombia and Thailand." *International Review of Applied Economics* 27, no. 3, pp. 386–404.

Coory, Phillip (2012) "Opposition divided over station sale." *Sydney Morning Herald*, 4 September. www.smh.com.

Cranston, Matthew (2012) "Chinese want slice of rural Australia." *Australian Financial Review*, 23 January.

Cross, Mai'A. K. Davis (2013) "Rethinking epistemic communities twenty years later." *Review of International Studies* 39, no. 1, pp. 137–160.

Crowe, David (2012) "Barnaby Joyce digs in on Cubbie as Coalition fractures over foreign deals." *The Australian*, 5 September. www.theaustralian.com.au.

Das, Sanchita Basu (2016) "Trade agreements are in ASEAN's best interests." *East Asia Forum*, 6 February. www.eastasiaforum.org.

Daugbjerg, Carsten, and Alan Swinbank (2009) *Ideas, Institutions, and Trade: The WTO and the Curious Role of EU Farm Policy in Trade Liberalization*. Oxford: Oxford University Press.

Davis, Bob (2011) "In trade talks, U.S. targets state subsidies." *Wall Street Journal*, 26 October. http://online.wsj.com.

de la Merced, Michael J. (2013) "U.S. security panel clears a Chinese takeover of Smithfield Foods." *New York Times,* 6 September. http://dealbook.nytimes.com.

Dent, Christopher (2008) *East Asian Regionalism.* Oxford: Routledge.

de Rosenzweig, Francisco (2012) "México en el tpp: Una ventana hacia el futuro." Geneva: International Centre for Trade and Sustainable Development, 12 August. www.ictsd.org/bridges-news/puentes/news/m%C3%A9xico-en-el-tpp-una-ventana-hacia-el-futuro.

Donilon, Tom (2013) "Press briefing by National Security Advisor Tom Donilon." 8 June. www.whitehouse.gov/the-press-office/2013/06/08/press-briefing-national-security-advisor-tom-donilon.

Drake-Brockman, Jane (2013) "Could China end the WTO's 'big nothing' in services reform?" *East Asia Forum,* 29 October. www.eastasiaforum.org.

Drysdale, Peter (2013) "Asian trade strategies." *East Asia Forum,* 29 September. www.eastasiaforum.org.

Dube, Ryan (2013) "The Pacific Alliance: Market-friendly integration." *Latin Trade,* 18 May. http://latintrade.com.

Duina, Francesco G. (2006) *The Social Construction of Free Trade: The European Union, NAFTA, and MERCOSUR.* Princeton: Princeton University Press.

Dussel Peters, Enrique, Adrian H. Hearn, and Harley S. Shaiken (eds.) (2013) *China and the New Triangular Relationships in the Americas: China and the Future of U.S.-Mexico Relations.* Berkeley: University of California–Berkeley Center for Latin American Studies.

The Economist (2011) "Food safety in China: In the gutter." 29 October.

——— (2013) "Latin American geoeconomics: A continental divide."

——— (2014) "Bailing out from Bali." 9 August.

El Economista (2014) "Alianza del Pacífico será selectiva." 23 January. http://eleconomista.com.

Elek, Andrew (2015) "China takes the lead on economic integration." *East Asia Forum,* 7 July. www.eastasiaforum.org.

Ellefson, Wayne, Lorna Zach, and Darryl Sullivan (eds.) (2013) *Improving Import Food Safety.* Oxford: Blackwell.

Ellis, R. Evan (2009) *China in Latin America: The Whats and Wherefores.* Boulder: Lynne Rienner.

Eslake, Saul (2011). "The counterexample of Australia." In *What's Next?* edited by David Hale and Lyric Hale, pp. 139–150. New Haven: Yale University Press.

Estadão (2010) "China compra terras no Brasil." 3 August. http://opiniao.estadao.com.

Fellet, João (2011) "Comercio Brasil-China bate recorde, mas peso de commodities preocupa governo." *BBC Brasil,* 12 April. www.bbc.co.uk.

Ferguson, Doug, and Hans Hendrischke (2013) *Demystifying Chinese Investment in Australian Agribusiness.* Sydney: KPMG and University of Sydney.

Ferguson, Doug, Hans Hendrischke, and Vaughn Barber (2014) *Demystifying SOE Investment in Australia.* Sydney: KPMG and University of Sydney.

Fergusson, Ian F., William H. Cooper, Remy Jurenas, and Brock R. Williams (2013) *The Trans-Pacific Partnership Negotiations and Issues for Congress.* Washington, DC: Congressional Research Service.

Fitzpatrick Behrens, Susan (2009) "Plan Mexico and Central America migration." *NACLA Report on the Americas,* 12 January. https://nacla.org.

Flynn, Sean, Margot E. Kaminski, Brook K. Baker, and Jimmy H. Koo (2011) "Public interest analysis of the US TPP proposal for an IP chapter." Research Paper no. 21. Washington, DC: Program on Information Justice and Intellectual Property.

Fraser, Andrew, and Sarah Elks (2011) "Great Tully sugar sell-off proves bittersweet." *The Australian,* 6 July. www.theaustralian.com.

Freidberg, Susanne (2004) *French Beans and Food Scares: Culture and Commerce in an Anxious Age*. New York: Oxford University Press.

Frost, Ellen (2013) "Strategic implications of TPP: Answering the critics." *Asia Pacific Bulletin* no. 220 (9 July). Honolulu, HI: East-West Center. www.eastwestcenter.org.

Fukunaga, Yoshifumi, and Ikumo Isono (2013) "Taking ASEAN+1 FTAs towards the RCEP: A mapping study." Discussion Paper no. ERIA-DP-2013-02. Jakarta: Economic Research Institute for ASEAN and East Asia (ERIA). www.eria.org.

GAIN (Global Agricultural Information Network) (2010) *National Plan for Expansion of Grain Production Capacity by 50 Billion Kilograms (2009–2020)*. Unofficial translation. Washington, DC: USDA Foreign Agricultural Service.

Gale, Fred, and Jean C. Buzby (2009) "Imports from China and food safety issues." *Economic Information Bulletin* no. 52 (July). Washington, DC: US Department of Agriculture. www.ers.usda.gov.

Gallagher, Kevin P. (2011) "Losing control: Policy space for capital controls in trade and investment agreements." *Development Policy Review* 29, no. 4, pp. 387–413.

——— (2015) "Obama abandons allies on China's Marshall Plan." *The Globalist,* 18 March. www.theglobalist.com.

Gallagher, Kevin P., and Margaret Myers (2014) *China–Latin America Finance Database*. Washington, DC: Inter-American Dialogue.

Gallagher, Kevin P., and Leonardo Stanley (2012) *Global Financial Reform and Trade Rules: The Need for Reconciliation*. Boston: Boston University, Pardee Task Force on Regulating Capital Flows.

——— (2013) *Capital Account Regulations and the Trading System: A Compatibility Review*. Boston: Boston University, Pardee Task Force on Regulating Capital Flows.

Garnaut, John (2012) "Abbott talks tough during China visit." *Sydney Morning Herald,* 25 July. www.smh.com.au.

Gelpern, Ann, and Brad Setser (2004) "Domestic and external debt: The doomed quest for equal treatment." *Georgetown Journal of International Law* 35, no. 4, pp. 795–814.

Gewertz, Deborah B., and Frederick Karl Errington (2010) *Cheap Meat: Flap Food Nations in the Pacific Islands*. Berkeley: University of California Press.

Ghitter, Geoff, and Alan Smart (2009) "Mad cows, regional governance, and urban sprawl: Path dependence and unintended consequences in the Calgary region." *Urban Affairs Review* 44, pp. 617–644.

Global Times (2013a) "China could have key role to play in TPP." 28 November. www.globaltimes.cn.

——— (2013b) "Chinese imports to hit $10 trillion by 2018." 17 March. http://gbtimes.com.

Goh, Evelyn (2013) *The Struggle for Order: Hegemony, Hierarchy, and Transition in Post–Cold War East Asia*. New York: Oxford University Press.

Goldfarb, Zachary A. (2015) "What Elizabeth Warren would say in her stump speech—if she runs for president." *Washington Post,* 7 January. www.washingtonpost.com.

Goto, Shihoko (2015) "Could the TPP actually divide Asia?" *The Diplomat,* 22 October. http://thediplomat.com.

Government of Canada (2012) "Government of Canada Releases Policy Statement and Revised Guidelines for Investments by State-Owned Enterprises." *Market Wired*, 7 December. www.marketwired.com.

Gray, Jamie (2013) "Chinese dairy giant enters NZ market with $210m factory." *New Zealand Herald*, 5 February. www.nzherald.co.nz.

Haas, Peter (1992) "Introduction: Epistemic communities and international policy coordination." *International Organization* 46, no. 1, pp. 1–35.

Hagan, Sean (2000) *Transfer of Funds*. New York: United Nations Conference on Trade and Development. www.unctad.org/en/docs/psiteiitd20.en.pdf.

He, Luan (2012) "RCEP Duikang TPP Shige Weimingti" (RCEP competing with the TPP: A false statement). *China Trade News*, 6 December, pp. 7–8.

He, Yafei (2015) "China sees a chance in TPP to stimulate reforms." *China-US Focus*, 23 October. www.chinausfocus.com.

Hearn, Adrian H. (2012) "Cuba and China: In mixed enterprise we trust." *Hemisphere* 21 (July), pp. 20–22.

——— (2013a) "China and Brazil: Searching for sustainable complementarity." Policy paper for the Europe China Research and Advice Network (ECRAN), European Commission. London: ECRAN.

——— (2013b) "China changes tack on trade and the TPP." *Australian Financial Review*, 5 June.

Henton, Darcy (2013) "Ralph Klein—the Teflon premier—and his nine lives." *Calgary Herald*, 28 March. www.calgaryherald.com.

Heritage Foundation (2015) *China Investment Tracker*. www.heritage.org/research/projects/china-global-investment-tracker-interactive-map.

Herreros, Sebastián (2011) *The Trans-Pacific Strategic Economic Partnership Agreement: A Latin American Perspective*. Santiago: Economic Commission for Latin America.

Hess, Ashley (2013) "Korea should stay out of the TPP—for now." *The Diplomat*, 5 September. http://thediplomat.com.

Hiebert, Murray, and Liam Hanlon (2012) "ASEAN and Partners Launch Regional Comprehensive Economic Partnership." December. http://csis.org/publication/asean-and-partners-launch-regional-comprehensive-economic-partnership.

Hiep, Le Hong (2013) "The U.S.-Vietnam comprehensive partnership: Key issues and implications." *East Asia Forum*, 6 August. www.eastasiaforum.org.

Hirschfeld Davis, Julie (2015) "Democrats step up efforts to block Obama's trade agenda." *New York Times*, 8 January. www.nytimes.com.

Hu, Weijia (2012) "Zhong Ri Han FTA Fan Xin" (China–Japan–South Korea FTA making new progress). *Hexun Wang News*, 3 December. http://news.hexun.com.

Huang, Yiping (2014) "Averting economic cold war." *East Asia Forum*, 19 January. www.eastasiaforum.org.

IADB (Inter-American Development Bank) (2012) "Guiding principles and objectives for negotiating the Regional Comprehensive Economic Partnership." Washington, DC: Inter-American Development Bank, August. www.iadb.org/intal/intalcdi/PE/CM%202013/11581.pdf.

IMF (International Monetary Fund) (2012a) *The Liberalization and Management of Capital Flows: An Institutional View*. Washington, DC.

——— (2012b) *Liberalizing Capital Flows and Managing Outflows*. Washington, DC.

——— (2014) *IMF Primary Commodity Prices Database*. www.imf.org/external/np/res/commod/index.aspx.

Irwin, Amos (2014) "Crossing the ocean by feeling for the BITs: Investor-state arbitration in China's bilateral investment treaties." GEGI Working Paper Series. www.bu.edu/pardee/research/global-economic-governance-2/chinabits.

Irwin, Douglas A. (1989) "Political economy and Peel's repeal of the Corn Laws." *Economics and Politics* 1, pp. 41–59.

Jackson, Andrew, and Matthew Sanger (1998) *Dismantling Democracy: The Multilateral Agreement on Investment (MAI) and Its Impact.* Ottawa: Canadian Centre for Policy Alternatives.

Japan Times (2013) "TPP sides set to keep food safety regimes." 28 August. www.japantimes.co.jp.

——— (2014) "APEC pushes road map by yearend for new Asia-Pacific free trade zone." 18 May. www.japantimes.co.jp.

Jiang Shixue (2011) "Ten key questions." In *China Engages Latin America: Tracing the Trajectory,* edited by Adrian H. Hearn and José Luis León-Manríquez, pp. 51–65. Boulder: Lynne Rienner.

Jiji (2015) "TPP to have 'limited' impact on 21 agricultural items, ministry says." *Japan Times,* 30 October. www.japantimes.co.jp.

Jin, Jianmin (2013) "RCEP vs. TPP." http://jp.fujitsu.com/group/fri/en/column/message/2013/2013-02-22.html.

Johnston, Eric (2013) "Hokkaido opposition to TPP surges." *Japan Times,* 10 April.

Kelly, Joe, and Sid Maher (2013) "Truss inflames Coalition rift over GrainCorp sale." *The Australian,* 4 November.

Kenny, Mark, and Philip Wen (2014) "Tony Abbott briefs Xi Jinping on search for MH370." *Sydney Morning Herald,* 11 April. www.smh.com.au.

Kesavan, K. V., and Kartikeya Khanna (2012) "Japan's dilemma on the Trans-Pacific Partnership: Analysis." *Eurasia Review,* 11 September. www.eurasiareview.com.

Kimball, Anne M. (2006) *Risky Trade: Infectious Disease in the Era of Global Trade.* Burlington, VT: Ashgate.

Kindleberger, Charles (1973). *The World in Depression, 1929–1939.* Berkeley: University of California Press.

Krist, William (2012) "Negotiations for a Trans-Pacific Partnership agreement." Washington, DC: Woodrow Wilson Center. www.wilsoncenter.org/sites/default/files/PAGE_TPP_REPORT.pdf.

Kurlantzick, Joshua (2008) "China's growing influence in Southeast Asia." In *China's Expansion into the Western Hemisphere,* edited by Riordan Roett and Guadalupe Paz, pp. 193–212. Washington, DC: Brookings Institution Press.

Lake, Marilyn (2010) "'Yellow peril' racism rears its ugly head." *Sydney Morning Herald,* 3 April.

Landim, Raquel (2012a) "China freia e preço de minerio desaba." *Estadão,* 7 May. www.estadao.com.br.

——— (2012b) "Dilma deveria ser mais rapida e agressiva." *Estadão,* 7 May. www.estadao.com.br.

Lang, Tim, and Michael Heasman (2004) *Food Wars: The Global Battle for Mouths, Minds, and Markets.* London: Earthscan.

LAPOP (Latin American Public Opinion Project) (2014) *Brazil Country Data.* http://lapop.ccp.ucr.ac.cr/Lapop_English.html.

Larsen, Ken (2005) "Alberta's thirty years war against the family farm." In *The Return of the Trojan Horse: Alberta and the New World (Dis)Order,* edited by Trevor Harrison, pp. 190–212. Montreal: Black Rose.

Larum, John (2013) "Chinese perspectives on investing in Australia." Sydney: Lowy Institute for International Policy.

Lawson, Sandra, David Heacock, and Anna Stupnystka (2007) "Beyond the BRICS: A look at the 'next 11.'" In *BRICS and Beyond,* edited by Jim O'Neill. New York: Goldman Sachs.

Li, Lilian (2007) *Fighting Famine in North China.* Stanford: Stanford University Press.

Li, Luosha (2013) "Joining TPP at an appropriate time and of our own accord serves China's strategic interests." *China-US Focus,* 20 November. www.chinausfocus.com.

Li, Xiangyang (2012) "TPP, Zhongguo Jueqi Guocheng Zhong De Zhongda Tiaozhan" (TPP: A serious challenge for China's rise). *Guoji Jingji Pinglun* (International Economic Review) no. 2, pp. 17–27.

Liberal National Party of Australia (2012) *The Coalition's Policy Discussion Paper on Foreign Investment in Australian Agricultural Land and Agribusiness.* Canberra.

Lim, C. L., Deborah Elms, and Patrick Low (2012) *The Trans-Pacific Partnership: A Quest for a Twenty-First-Century Agreement.* Cambridge: Cambridge University Press.

Lind, Dara (2015) "The TPP's impact on agriculture, explained in 6 products." November 10. www.vox.com/policy-and-politics/2015/11/10/9704368/tpp-agriculture-food-safety.

Lindert, Peter, and Jeffrey Williamson (2003) "Does globalization make the world more unequal?" In *Globalization in Historical Perspective,* edited by Michael D. Bordo et al., pp. 227–276. Chicago: University of Chicago Press.

Ling, Huawei (2013) "Xin xingshi xia duiwai kaifang de zhanlue buju: Ziben xiangmu kaifang bushi jishu wenti" (The new situation of strategic opening: Capital account liberalization is not a technical problem). *Caixin Online,* 20 May. http://finance.caixin.com.

Lowy Institute for International Policy (2014) *Lowy Institute Poll 2014.* www.lowyinstitute.org/publications/lowy-institute-poll-2014.

Maciel, Rodrigo T., and Dani K. Nedal (2011) "China and Brazil: Two trajectories of a 'strategic partnership.'" In *China Engages Latin America: Tracing the Trajectory,* edited by Adrian H. Hearn and José Luis León-Manríquez, pp. 235–255. Boulder: Lynne Rienner.

Magud, Nicholas, and Carmen M. Reinhart (2006) *Capital Controls: An Evaluation.* NBER Working Paper no. 11973. www.nber.org/papers/w11973.

Marsden, Terry, and Roberta Sonnino (2005) "Rural development and agri-food governance in Europe: Tracing the development of alternatives." In *Agricultural Governance: Globalization and the New Politics of Regulation,* edited by Vaughan Higgins and Geoffrey Lawrence, pp. 50–68. New York: Routledge.

Martínez Pacheco, Selene (2014) *Chinese "Loan-for-Oil" Deals in Brazil, Venezuela, and Ecuador: Local Concerns and Perceptions.* PhD thesis. Sydney: University of Technology, Faculty of Arts and Social Sciences.

Menon, Jayant (2013) "The challenge facing Asia's Regional Comprehensive Economic Partnership." *East Asia Forum,* 23 June. www.eastasiaforum.org.

Morgan, Kevin, Terry Marsden, and Jonathan Murdoch (2006) *Worlds of Food: Place, Power, and Provenance in the Food Chain.* Oxford: Oxford University Press.

Mulgan, Aurelia George (2015) "What does the TPP mean for Japan's agricultural sector?" *East Asia Forum,* 19 November. www.eastasiaforum.org.

Muller, Birgit (2008) "Still feeding the world? The political ecology of Canadian prairie farmers." *Anthropologica* 50, pp. 389–407.

Murillo, María Victoria, Virginia Oliveros, and Milan Vaishnav (2011) "Economic constraints and presidential agency." In *The Resurgence of the Latin American Left*, edited by Steven Levitsky and Kenneth Roberts, pp. 52–70. Baltimore: Johns Hopkins University Press.

Murray, Lisa, and Angus Grigg (2013) "China's Wu Puingai eyes $700m Perth property play." *Australian Financial Review*, 22 April.

Myers, John F., and Mary H. Myers (1985) "The elephant and the mouse: Canada and the United States." *Bridgewater Review* 3, pp. 12–15.

NDRC (National Development and Reform Commission of China) (2013) *Report on the Implementation of the 2012 Plan for National Economic and Social Development and on the 2013 Draft Plan for National Economic and Social Development*. Beijing.

Neales, Sue (2012) "All sweet at Tully sugar mill as takeover fears vanish." *The Australian*, 29 October.

Noiville, Christine (2006) "Compatibility or clash? EU food safety and the WTO." In *What's the Beef? The Contested Governance of European Food Safety and the WTO*, edited by Christopher K. Ansell and David Vogel, pp. 307–325. Cambridge, MA: MIT Press.

OECD (Organization for Economic Cooperation and Development) (2012) "Competitive neutrality: Maintaining a level playing field between public and private business." www.oecd.org/daf/ca/corporategovernanceofstate-ownedenterprises/50302961.pdf.

——— (2013) *Perspectives on Global Development 2013: Industrial Policies in a Changing World*. Paris: OECD Publishing.

Oliveira, Francisco (2006) "Lula in the Labyrinth." *New Left Review* 42, pp. 5–22.

O'Neill, Jim, Dominic Wilson, Roopa Purushothaman, and Anna Stupnytska (2005) "How solid are the BRICs?" www.goldmansachs.com/our-thinking/archive/how-solid.html.

Ostry, Jonathan D., et al. (2010) *Capital Inflows: The Role of Controls*. IMF Staff Position Note No. 2010/04. www.imf.org/external/pubs/ft/spn/2010/spn1004.pdf.

Patel, Raj (2008) *Stuffed and Starved: Markets, Power, and the Hidden Battle for the World's Food System*. Toronto: HarperCollins.

Patterson, Michael (2013) "Emerging markets era of outperformance is ending, Goldman says." *Bloomberg News*, 21 June. www.bloomberg.com.

Pearson, Daniel R. (2015) "Sugar and the TPP." 13 August. www.cato.org/blog/sugar-tpp.

Peine, Emelie, and Philip McMichael (2005) "Globalization and global governance." In *Agricultural Governance: Globalization and the New Politics of Regulation*, edited by Vaughan Higgins and Geoffrey Lawrence, pp. 19–34. New York: Routledge.

Perú 21 (2013) "Bachelet enfriaría la Alianza Del Pacífico." 17 December. http://peru21.pe.

Petri, Peter A., and Michael G. Plummer (2012) "The Trans-Pacific Partnership and Asia-Pacific integration: Policy implications." Policy Brief no. 12-16. Washington, DC: Peterson Institute for International Economics. www.iie.com/publications/interstitial.cfm?ResearchID=2146.

Petri, Peter A., Michael G. Plummer, and Fan Zhai (2012) *The Trans-Pacific Partnership and Asia-Pacific Integration*. Policy Analyses in International Economics no. 98. Washington, DC: Peterson Institute for International Economics, November.

Pierson, David (2013) "Smithfield Foods shareholders approve Chinese purchase." *Los Angeles Times,* 24 September. www.latimes.com.

Pilling, David (2013) "It won't be easy to build an 'anyone but China' club." *Financial Times,* 22 May. www.ft.com.

Posen, Adam (2014) "A win-win solution for the TPP." *Caixin Online,* 13 June. http://english.caixin.com.

Powell, Dawn (2011) "The dragon's appetite for soy stokes Brazilian protectionism." *Financial Times,* 10 October. www.ft.com.

Prebisch, Raúl (1950) *The Economic Development of Latin America and Its Principal Problems.* New York: United Nations.

Pyne, Solana (2010) "China's Brazilian shopping spree." *Global Post,* 22 November. www.globalpost.com.

Qian, Liwei (2013) "Double implications of President Xi Jinping's Southeast Asia tour." *China-US Focus,* 12 October. www.chinausfocus.com.

Rehder, Marcelo, and David Friedlander (2010) "E preciso restringir o investimento chines no Brasil." *Estadão,* 22 August. www.estadao.com.br.

Roggeveen, Sam (2015) "Ashton Carter on the TPP and rebalance." *Lowy Interpreter,* 7 April. www.lowyinterpreter.org.

Ross, John (2011) "Realities behind the Trans-Pacific Partnership." 18 November. www.china.org.cn/opinion/2011-11/18/content_23953374.htm.

Salacuse, Jeswald W. (2010) *The Law of Investment Treaties.* Oxford: Oxford University Press.

Sautman, Barry, and Yan Hairong (2007) "Friends and interests: China's distinctive links with Africa." *African Studies Review* 50, no. 3, pp. 75–114.

——— (2008) "The forest for the trees: Trade, investment, and the China-in-Africa discourse." *Pacific Affairs* 81, no. 1, pp. 9–29.

——— (2009) "African perspectives on China-Africa links." *China Quarterly* 199, pp. 729–760.

Schneider, Carlos Rodolfo (2012) "Miopias do modelo de desenvolvimiento." *Estadão,* 5 May. www.estadao.com.br.

Schott, Jeffrey J. (2009) *Roadmap for the FTAAP: Take the TPP Turnpike.* Peterson Institute for International Economics presentation at APEC Japan 2010 Symposium, Tokyo, 9 December.

Schott, Jeffrey J., Barbara Kotschwar, and Julia Muir (2013) *Understanding the Trans-Pacific Partnership.* Policy Analyses in International Economics no. 99. Washington, DC: Peterson Institute for International Economics.

Schott, Jeffrey J., and Sean Miner (2015) "U.S.-China trade relations: Projecting the path forward." In *China's Economic Transformation: Lessons, Impact, and the Path Forward,* Briefing Series no. 15-3, pp. 7–16. Washington, DC: Peterson Institute for International Economics.

Scissors, Derek (2013a) "China's global investment rises: The U.S. should focus on competition." *Heritage Foundation Backgrounder* no. 2757 (8 January).

——— (2013b) "Why the Trans-Pacific Partnership must enhance competitive neutrality." Trade Backgrounder no. 2809. Washington, DC: Heritage Foundation.

Selden, Mark (2012) "Economic nationalism and regionalism in contemporary East Asia." *Asia-Pacific Journal,* issue 43, vol. 10, no. 2. http://japanfocus.org/-Mark-Selden/3848.

Severino, Rodolfo (2012) "ASEAN's role in East Asian regionalism: Manager or leader?" Paper delivered at the conference "Emerging Regionalism: Paradigm

Shift of International Relations in East Asia?" Chinese University of Hong Kong, 9 March. www.cuhk.edu.hk/hkiaps/conference/Mar2012/download/Ambassador_Rodolfo.pdf.

Sinha, Rohit, and Geethanjali Nataraj (2013) "Regional Comprehensive Economic Partnership (RCEP): Issues and way forward." *The Diplomat,* 30 July. http://thediplomat.com.

Skogstad, Grace (2008) *Internationalization and Canadian Agriculture: Policy and Governing Paradigms.* Toronto: University of Toronto Press.

Smart, Alan, and Josephine Smart (2009) "Learning from disaster? Mad cows, squatter fires, and institutional learning." In *The Political Economy of Hazards and Disasters,* edited by Eric C. Jones and Arthur D. Murphy, pp. 267–293. Lanham: Altamira.

——— (2012a) "Governing beef: Program implementation, unintended consequences, and BSE control in Alberta." In *Governing Cultures: Anthropological Perspectives on Political Labor, Power, and Government,* edited by Kendra Coulter and William R. Schumann, pp. 69–92. New York: Palgrave Macmillan.

——— (2012b) "Hong Kong petty capitalists investing in China: Risk tolerance, uncertain investment environments, success and failure." In *Globalization from Below: The World's Other Economy,* edited by Gordon Mathews, Gustavo Lin Ribeiro, and Carlos Alba Vega, pp. 103–119. New York: Routledge.

——— (2012c) "Quarantine, biosecurity, and life across the border." In *A Companion to Border Studies,* edited by Thomas M. Wilson and Hastings Donnan, pp. 354–370. New York: Wiley-Blackwell.

Song, Guoyou, and Wen Jin Yuan (2012) "China's free trade agreement strategies." *Washington Quarterly* (Fall). http://csis.org/files/publication/twq12FallSongYuan.pdf.

Song, Yinghui (2013) "Keeping regional economies working together." *East Asia Forum,* 25 October. www.eastasiaforum.org.

Spriggs, John, and Grant E. Isaac (2001) *Food Safety and International Competitiveness: The Case of Beef.* Wallingford, UK: CABI Publishing.

Stadius, Eric, and Elizabeth Briggs (2012) "The Trans-Pacific Partnership: Free trade at what costs?" *COHA Report,* 20 August. Washington, DC: Council on Hemispheric Affairs. www.coha.org/the-trans-pacific-partnership-free-trade-at-what-costs.

State Council of China (2012) "Zhong-Ri-Han Sanguo Jingmao Buzhang Juxing Huiwu: Qidong Sanguo Zimaoqu Tanpan" (Economic and trade ministers of China, Japan, and Korea meet and launch negotiations for a free trade zone between the three countries). 20 November. www.gov.cn/gzdt/2012-11/20/content_2271477.htm.

——— (2014) "Guowuyuan bangongting guanyu jiakuai fazhan shangye jiankangbaoxian de ruogan yijian" (Opinions on promotion of health service sector development). *Guo Ban Fa* no. 50 (17 November). http://news.xinhuanet.com/fortune/2014-11/17/c_1113279221.htm.

Steffensen, Jennifer (2013) "New dynamics in US global trade strategy? A reinvigorated Japan and the Trans-Pacific Partnership—a roundtable report." Washington, DC: National Bureau of Asian Research.

Su, Xiaohui (2012) "Developments and prospects of the RCEP." 27 November. www.ciis.org.cn/english/2012-11/27/content_5529073.htm.

Sugarawa, Junichi (2007) *The FTAAP and Economic Integration in East Asia: Japan's Approach to Regionalism and US Engagement in East Asia.* Tokyo: Mizuho Research Institute, February.

Summers, Tim (2013) *Yunnan: A Chinese Bridgehead to Asia—A Case Study of China's Political and Economic Relations with Its Neighbours*. Cambridge: Chandos.

——— (2016) "China's 'new Silk Roads': Sub-national regions and networks of global political economy." *Third World Quarterly*, March.

Sutherlin, Laurel (2012) "What you need to know about a worldwide corporate power grab of enormous proportions." 11 September. www.alternet.org.

Taylor, John (2003) "Financial Services and Capital Transfer Provisions in Recent Free Trade Agreements." Testimony before the Subcommittee on Domestic and International Monetary Policy, Trade and Technology Committee on Financial Services, US House of Representatives. Washington, DC, 1 April. www.stanford.edu/~johntayl/taylorspeeches/Financial%20Services%20and%20Capital%20Transfer%20Provisions%20(1%20Apr%2003).doc.

Trevisani, Paulo, and Rogerio Jelmayer (2014) "China looking to play larger role in funding Brazil's infrastructure." *Wall Street Journal*, 13 July. www.wsj.com.

UIBE (University of International Business and Economics) (2013) "RCEP and TPP International Academic Forum held in UIBE." 10 December. http://english.uibe.edu.cn/International/NEWS/251917.jsp.

UN Comtrade (2016) *United Nations Commodity Trade Statistics Database*. http://comtrade.un.org/db/default.aspx.

ations Conference on Trade and Development) (2014) *World Investment Report*. Geneva.

UN-ECLAC (United Nations Economic Commission for Latin America and the Caribbean) (2012) "Latin America and the Caribbean in the world economy: Continuing crisis in the centre and opportunities for developing economies." Santiago.

UNCTAD (United NUS Census Bureau (2015) "Trade in goods with China." https://www.census.gov /foreign-trade/balance/c5700.html.

US Department of State (2010) *Model Bi-Lateral Investment Treaty*. Washington, DC: Department of State.

USTR (United States Trade Representative) (2004) *US-Model BIT*. Washington, DC.

——— (2011) "The United States in the Trans-Pacific Partnership." www.ustr.gov/about-us/press-office/fact-sheets/2011/november/united-states-trans-pacific-partnership.

——— (2015) "Outlines of TPP." USTR Executive Office of the President. https://ustr.gov/tpp/outlines-of-TPP.

Viterbo, Anna Maria (2012) *International Economic Law and Monetary Measures, Limitations to States' Sovereignty, and Dispute Settlement*. London: Edward Elgar.

Wang, Yi (2013) "Yatai Ying Cheng ZhongMei Goujian Xinxing Guanxi Shiyantian." (Asia-Pacific should become the testing ground for building a new type of US-China relationship). Speech to Brookings Institution, Washington, DC, 21 September.

Wang, Yuzhu (2013) "The RCEP Initiative and ASEAN 'centrality.'" *China International Studies* (September–October). www.ciis.org.cn/english/2013-12/06/content_6518129.htm.

Watkins, Mel (1985) "Multinationals, branch plants, and Canada-US relations." In *The New Practical Guide to Canadian Political Economy*, edited by Daniel Drache and Wallace Clement, pp. 93–101. Toronto: Lorimer.

Weis, Tony (2007) *The Global Food Economy: The Battle for the Future of Farming*. London: Zed.

Weissmann, Jordan (2015) "Is it possible Donald Trump was right about China and the TPP?" *Slate Online*, 11 November. www.slate.com.

Wentzel, Marina (2010) "Brasil deve fomentar cooperação e evitar controvérsias com a China, dizem analistas." *BBC Brazil*, 17 November. www.bbc.co.uk/portuguese/noticias.

White, Leslie (2012) "China set to claim land in northern Aus." *Weekly Times Now*, 16 May. www.weeklytimesnow.com.au.

White House (2015) "Weekly Address: We Should Make Sure the Future Is Written by Us." White House Office of the Press Secretary, 21 February. www.whitehouse.gov/the-press-office/2015/02/21/weekly-address-we-should-make-sure-future-written-us.

——— (2016) "Remarks of President Barack Obama: State of the Union address as delivered." Press release, January 12. www.whitehouse.gov/sotu.

Wilson, Dominic, Alex Kelston, and Swamali Ahmed (2010) "Is this the 'BRICs Decade'?" *BRICs Monthly* 10, no. 3. www.goldmansachs.com/our-thinking/archive/brics-decade.html.

Winter, Brian, and Caroline Stauffer (2013) "Insight: Chinese investors sour on Brazil, and projects melt away." *Reuters*, 1 November.

World Bank (2014) "GDP at market prices (current US$)." http://data.worldbank.org/indicator/NY.GDP.MKTP.CD?end=2014&start=1960&view=chart.

World Economic Forum (2013a) "Global Agenda Survey 2012." *World Economic Forum Reports*. http://reports.weforum.org/global-agenda-survey-2012/trends/rise-of-emerging-economies.

——— (2013b) "Premier Li Keqiang predicts smooth sailing for Chinese economy." 12 September. www.weforum.org.

Wu, Guoguang (ed.) (2007) *China Turns to Multilateralism: Foreign Policy and Regional Security*. Florence, KY: Routledge.

Xi, Jinping (2013) "Shenhua Gaige Kaifang, Gongchuang Meihao Yatai" (Deepening reform and opening up to build a pleasant Asia-Pacific together). Speech to APEC forum of business leaders, 7 October. *People's Daily*, 8 October.

Xinhua News (2013) "Closer China-ASEAN economic ties despite disputes." 5 September. http://news.xinhuanet.com.

——— (2014a) "China unveils landmark urbanization plan." 16 March. http://news.xinhuanet.com.

——— (2014b) "Full text of Li Keqiang's speech at opening ceremony of Boao Forum." 10 April. http://news.xinhuanet.com.

——— (2015) "TPP, key deal for Asia-Pacific: China's MOC." 6 October. http://news.xinhuanet.com.

Xinmin News (2013) "Indonesia may prefer RCEP to TPP." 30 January. http://fashion.xinmin.cn.

Yahuda, Michael (2007) "China's multilateralism and regional order." In *China Turns to Multilateralism: Foreign Policy and Regional Security*, edited by Wu Guoguang, pp. 75–89. Florence, KY: Routledge.

Yan, Hairong, and Barry Sautman (2010) "Chinese firms in Zambia: From Socialist to Anglo-Imperialist engagement?" *African and Asian Studies* 9, pp. 307–333.

Yang, Jiang (2008) "Australia-China FTA: China's domestic politics and the roots of different national approaches to FTAs." *Australian Journal of International Affairs* 62, no. 2, pp. 179–195.

Yang, Yi (2013) "U.S. Asia-Pacific alliance and China's regional strategy." *International Security Research* (Chinese) 3, pp. 127–259.

Ye, Shulan (2010) "China's regional policy in East Asia and its characteristics." University of Nottingham China Policy Institute Paper. www.chinapolicy institute.org.

Yu, Lintao (2012) "RCEP makes a difference." 27 November. www.china.org .cn/opinion/2012-11/27/content_27237543.htm.

Yuan, Wen Jin (2012) *The Trans-Pacific Partnership and China's Corresponding Strategies.* Freeman Briefing Report. Washington, DC: Center for Strategic and International Studies.

Yun, Sun (2015) "China and the changing Asian Infrastructure Bank." *PacNet* no. 43. http://csis.org/files/publication/Pac1543_0.pdf.

Zarroli, Jim (2015) "New Asian Development Bank seen as sign of China's growing influence." *National Public Radio* transcript. www.npr.org/2015/04/16/4001 78364/finance-officials-to-discuss-asian-development-bank-at-spring-meetings.

Zhang, Qizuo (2013) "Acceleration of TPP and TTIP by US: Ulterior motives and impact." *Guangming Daily,* 12 June.

Zhang, Yuanan, Chen Lixiong, and Chen Qin (2013) "Closer look: How agreements like the TPP press China to reform." *Caixin Online,* 30 October. http://english .caixin.com.

Zhang, Yunling (2009) *China and Asian Regionalism.* River Edge, NJ: World Scientific.

Zhou, Zhou (2014) "The road to FTAAP: RCEP or TPP?" *Daily News,* 19 May. http://money.163.com/14/0519/00/9SINTDA300253B0H.html?from=endart.

The Contributors

Ariel C. Armony is the University of Pittsburgh's senior director of international programs and director of the University Center for International Studies. He also holds faculty appointments in the Graduate School of Public and International Affairs and the Department of Political Science at the Dietrich School of Arts and Sciences. His extensive record of publications covers Latin American politics, democratization, and the relationship between Latin America and China.

Nashira P. Chávez is a PhD candidate at the University of Miami. Her research focuses on the intersection of foreign policy, economic power, oil, and politics in China–Latin America relations. Prior to joining the University of Miami she worked for the Ecuadorian government.

Kevin P. Gallagher is professor of global development policy at Boston University's Frederick S. Pardee School of Global Studies, where he codirects the Global Economic Governance Initiative and the Global Development Policy Program. His latest books are *The China Triangle: Latin America's China Boom and the Fate of the Washington Consensus* and *Ruling Capital: Emerging Markets and the Re-Regulation of Cross-Border Finance*.

Adrian H. Hearn is associate professor of Latin American studies at the University of Melbourne. An anthropologist by training, he consults for governmental and nongovernmental institutions on the health, food security, and social challenges arising from Asia Pacific economic integration. He is a recipient of the Díaz-Ayala Award from Florida International University and the Kiriyama Award from the University of San Francisco. His books include *Diaspora and Trust: Cuba, Mexico, and the Rise of China; China Engages Latin America: Tracing the Trajectory;* and *Cuba: Religion, Social Capital, and Development*.

Carla A. Hills is chairman and chief executive officer of Hills & Company International Consultants, which provides advice to international firms on investment, trade, and risk assessment abroad. Ambassador Hills served in the cabinets of President George H. W. Bush as US Trade Representative and of President Gerald R. Ford as secretary of the Department of Housing and Urban Development. She chairs the National Committee on US-China Relations and cochairs the Council on Foreign Relations, the Inter-American Dialogue, and the International Advisory Board of the Center for Strategic and International Studies. She is also a member of the Secretary of State's Foreign Affairs Policy Board.

Jianmin Jin is a senior fellow at the Fujitsu Research Institute, where he coordinates research on Asian emerging economies, regional integration, and strategies for multinational corporations; and visiting professor at Japan's Asia University. Among his books are *Free Trade and Environment Protection: Lessons from NAFTA; China's Leading Enterprises and Main Industries; The Turning Point of Japan-China Relations; China's Economic Reality: View from an Ethnic Chinese Economist;* and *India vs. China.*

Barbara Kotschwar is an adjunct professor of Latin American studies and economics at Georgetown University, where she teaches courses on political economy and trade and integration in the Americas. When she is not teaching at Georgetown, she is a senior investment policy officer in the Trade and Competitiveness Global Practice Unit at the World Bank. From 2007 to 2015 she was a research fellow with the Peterson Institute for International Economics. She is coeditor of *Trade Rules in the Making: Multilateral and Regional Trade Arrangements.*

Margaret Myers is director of the China and Latin America Program at the Inter-American Dialogue (IAD). She established the IAD's China and Latin America Working Group in 2011 to examine China's growing presence in Latin America and the Caribbean. Myers has published numerous articles on Chinese leadership dynamics, international capital flows, Chinese agricultural policy, and Asia–Latin America relations.

Alan Smart is professor in the Department of Anthropology and Archaeology at the University of Calgary. His research has focused on urban issues, housing, foreign investment, social change, food safety, zoonotic diseases, and agriculture in Hong Kong, China, and Canada. He is author of *Making Room: Squatter Clearance in Hong Kong; Petty Capitalists and Globalization* (coedited with Josephine Smart); *The Shek Kip Mei Myth: Squatters, Fires, and Colonial Rule in Hong Kong, 1950–1963;* and numerous articles in journals and edited volumes.

Josephine Smart is professor in the Department of Anthropology and Archaeology at the University of Calgary. Her research and teaching focus on economic anthropology, food production and zoonotic diseases, social and economic development in post-1978 China, Chinese international migration, immigrant entrepreneurs, and the international mobility of capital and labor. She is coeditor of *Petty Capitalists and Globalization: Flexibility, Entrepreneurship, and Economic Development* and *Plural Globalities in Multiple Localities: New World Borders,* and author of *The Political Economy of Street Hawkers in Hong Kong.*

Tim Summers is adjunct assistant professor at the Centre for China Studies, Chinese University of Hong Kong, and a nonresident senior consulting fellow at Chatham House. His research on the politics, political economy, and international relations of contemporary China has generated publications on China's new Silk Roads for *Third World Quarterly* and the book *Yunnan: A Chinese Bridgehead to*

Asia. Tim was a British diplomat for thirteen years, including a post as consul-general in Chongqing, China, from 2004 to 2007.

Zhang Xuegang is deputy director of the Institute for South Asia, Southeast Asia, and Oceania Studies at the China Institute of Contemporary International Relations in Beijing. His research interests include transpacific economic architecture, China-US-ASEAN relations, South China Sea issues, and Myanmar studies. Among his publications are *Maritime Security and International Cooperation* and regular contributions to the Jamestown Foundation's *China Brief*.

Index

About the Book

THIS COMPREHENSIVE ASSESSMENT OF TRANSPACIFIC ECONOMIC INTEgration explores the many ways that new approaches to multilateral cooperation, and notably the Trans-Pacific Partnership (TPP), are transforming the regional landscape.

Reflecting diverse views on the merits of new and wide-ranging agreements, the authors consider: To what extent will the TPP facilitate the US "pivot" to Asia at a time when China, not a TPP member, is attempting to shape regional economic dynamics? Will the Regional Comprehensive Economic Partnership, strongly backed by China, prove complementary or antagonistic to the TPP? How can countries throughout Latin America and Asia best secure benefits from emerging accords? As they engage with these and related issues/debates, they also provide informed assessments of the political and economic significance of the new agreements for the future of transpacific integration.

Adrian H. Hearn is associate professor of Latin American studies at the University of Melbourne. **Margaret Myers** is director of the China and Latin America Program at the Inter-American Dialogue.